tender: that which requires careful handling; soft and easily chewed; a softness or gentleness in one's relations with others; that which is expressive of warm affection, concern; to offer, to give; a means of payment; has or expresses affection, love, consideration; someone who tends

tender
FARMERS, COOKS, EATERS

Tamara Murphy
with
Marlen Boivin, Jody Ericson Dorow and Nancy Gellos

Photography: Angie Norwood Browne
Food Stylist: Patty Wittmann

ShinShinChez LLC
Seattle, WA

TENDER: farmers, cooks, eaters
Copyright 2010 Marlen Boivin, Jody Ericson Dorow, Nancy Gellos, Tamara Murphy

First edition 2010
Printed in Canada

Author: Tamara Murphy
Editorial Direction: Marlen Boivin, Jody Ericson Dorow, Nancy Gellos
Photographer: Angie Norwood Browne
Food Stylist: Patty Wittmann
Copy Editor: Judy Gouldthorpe
Project Management: Jody Ericson Dorow
Recipe Testing Coordination: Marlen Boivin
Design: Nancy Gellos
Publisher: ShinShinChez LLC

ISBN-10: 0982722508
ISBN-13: 978-0-9827225-0-3

ShinShinChez LLC
2212 Queen Anne Avenue North #334
Seattle, WA 98109
(206) 914-5886
email: info@shinshinchez.com
www.shinshinchez.com

This is our moment to remember we do have choices.

A meal at a time, we can make choices and MAKE A DIFFERENCE. This book is meant to inspire you to cook more. There are many cookbooks available to us with great recipes that send you to the store for this and that, which can turn into a wild-goose chase depending on where you live and what is in season. I believe that what grows together goes together. That we would be so much healthier and would also find that we are really much better in the kitchen than we think if we stick to a few rules and learn to cook within the seasons.

Our nation today has more choices than ever in regard to what lands on our tables, choices that leave us confused and baffled. This book is about stopping to consider what our choices are — and trying to make the best one. But we first need to get a little clearer on the choices we do have.

My work with local farms has continually increased over the years, and now mostly all the food at my restaurants, including pork, beef, and poultry, is purchased directly from the very farms where it was grown. I need these farmers and the food they raise in order to create and cook at a level that I am proud of. When I use their products I am confident that I am giving my customers the best. This can happen only if we have the freshest and best of what the seasons offer.

I have discovered that I cook differently now, and my hope is that these pages will bring you to a deeper understanding and awareness of our farmers' lives. I am 100 percent committed to supporting this effort to keep farms here, and thriving. I believe that buying from our local farms is simply the right thing to do.

Somehow I feel that this path found me — it chose me. Throughout my life, I have discovered my passion for food and learned to express my voice through food. That expression has allowed this expansion, a journey — with the connection between farmers, cooks, and eaters. Connections are intimate.

It is food that has allowed me to ponder this story. I've considered questions like "What is food?" "What is the circle of food among the farmers, the cooks, and the eaters?" and "What responsibility do we have to fight for food?" Some questions have answers, and some don't. Some questions just pose more questions.

My biggest hope is that this journey will help us remember how our food used to be grown and ignite a desire to become connected again with those who take care of our planet, to create great dishes, and to get to know those who enjoy both efforts.

Good health and well-being begin with having healthy relationships, with each other, our communities, and our planet. Cooking healthy and tasty meals for our friends and family is a great way to begin.

We want this collection of discoveries and recipes to inspire respect for one another and instill pride in all that we do. In this journey through the seasons, discover taste, texture, and color . . . discover a connection to our Earth, to people, and to animals. We learn as we go — have fun!

Tamara

Farm-Fresh Eggs

Farm-fresh eggs are a really different experience in comparison to store-bought. You can tell how fresh they are by how they sit in water. A fresh egg will lie on the bottom of a cup of water, while an older egg will float a bit.

How to Poach an Egg

Put 3 to 4 cups of water in a medium saucepan with 1 tablespoon of salt and 2 tablespoons of white wine vinegar. Bring it to a boil. While the water is heating, crack each egg into a holding cup. Reduce the heat to medium-low, and when the water is just simmering, gently add the eggs one at a time. Poach for approximately 2½ to 3 minutes, or until the egg white is fully cooked and the yolk appears set but is still loose. Remove with a slotted spoon to drain.

If you'd like to prepare them earlier in the day, place the poached eggs in an ice bath to hold for later use. You'll notice the egg yolk stiffening up as if it's overcooked. When you're ready to serve, place the poached eggs in simmering water for about 30 seconds to warm them through and they will loosen up.

After placing a raw egg in the simmering water, I like to swirl the water with the end of a spatula or a chopstick before adding the next one. The circular motion of the water will help the egg white take a round shape.

Wilted Frisée with Farm-Fresh Eggs
Serves 4 to 6

4 bacon slices
1 shallot, sliced
1 garlic clove, chopped
2 tablespoons sherry vinegar
1 teaspoon Dijon mustard
1 head of frisée, washed, leaves separated from the root
4-6 poached or fried farm eggs (1 per serving)
2 sprigs fresh thyme, leaves removed

Cook the bacon in a large skillet over medium heat until crispy. Remove with a slotted spoon, leaving the bacon fat in the pan.

Add the shallot and garlic to the pan and cook over low to medium heat until translucent. Stir in the vinegar and mustard.

Remove the pan from the heat and add the frisée. Toss in the pan, coating all the leaves.

Divide the frisée among individual plates and add crumbled bacon. Top each serving with a cooked egg. Sprinkle the thyme leaves over the salad.

Asparagus

When you buy
in-season asparagus
from your local farmers,
it's an entirely different
vegetable from what
you will find at the
grocery store out of
season. I eat as much
asparagus as I can while
it's here. It's good for
us and abundant in the
spring. Top it with a
beautiful poached fresh
chicken or duck egg and
it makes a perfect spring
lunch or light supper.
Figure on five to six large
spears per person.

Grilled Asparagus with Arugula, Poached Egg, and Pecorino
Serves 1

I really enjoy the taste of grilled asparagus. You can also roast it in the oven (see note). What I am looking for is a nice crispy texture on the outside. I'm all about cooking veggies as you like them — until *you* think they're done. If you like your vegetables softer, then cook them longer.

5-6 large asparagus spears
Extra-virgin olive oil
Salt
2 bamboo skewers, soaked in water for 30 minutes (optional)
Fresh lemon juice
Freshly ground black pepper
Handful of fresh arugula leaves
1 poached egg
Pecorino Romano or Parmigiano-Reggiano cheese
White truffle oil (optional)
Toasted baguette rubbed with fresh garlic, for serving

Preheat the grill.

Snap the woody ends off the asparagus. Brush with olive oil and season with a pinch of salt.

Lay the asparagus crosswise on the grill. Or, for easier grilling, you can stick one bamboo skewer perpendicularly through the root ends and the other through the tip ends, skewering all the spears together. Grill on medium heat for 5 to 8 minutes, or until tender.

Toss the grilled asparagus in a little olive oil and fresh lemon juice, then season to taste with salt and pepper.

Arrange the asparagus on a plate, add the arugula, and top with the poached egg. Grate fresh Pecorino Romano over the top and add a few grinds of pepper. If you have it, drizzle a little white truffle oil over the arugula. Serve with the toasted baguette.

Note: To roast the asparagus, preheat the oven to 350°F. Place the oiled and seasoned asparagus in a roasting pan, being sure not to crowd the pan. Roast for about 10 minutes, or until tender.

Sweetened Braised Rhubarb

Makes about 1 cup

The trick with rhubarb is to not cook it — you just want to steep it. First, cut it how you like it; I prefer a small dice. Then pour your boiling liquid over it to cover. Do this very gently and it will become tender, not mushy. Depending on what you're using it for, if you want a slightly thicker sauce — say for rhubarb compote — you can drain off the liquid and add a small amount of arrowroot. For this dish, we want the extra liquid. At the restaurants we also use this braised rhubarb in a bacon dressing served with duck for a salty, sweet, earthy combination.

1 cup fresh orange juice and grated zest
3-4 tablespoons sugar
1 tablespoon fresh thyme leaves
1 pound *peeled* rhubarb (this removes the bitter taste), diced
Salt and freshly ground black pepper
Pinch of arrowroot (optional)

Place the orange juice, zest, and sugar in a small saucepan. Bring to a boil over medium-low heat, stirring occasionally so the sugar is fully dissolved. Add the thyme. Remove from the heat.

Gently pour the hot liquid over the rhubarb, give it a gentle stir so it is fully immersed, and let it steep for about 8 minutes. It should be fork tender, but not mushy. Add a tiny bit of salt and some pepper.

If you want a thicker sauce, strain the rhubarb and set aside. Pour the liquid back into the saucepan, add more orange juice, and bring to a simmer. Stir in the arrowroot.

Try adding chopped crisp bacon to your rhubarb sauce for a savory twist.

A little cranberry or pomegranate juice in addition to or instead of OJ is a nice touch, and adds color.

Shopping in the farmers' market and choosing this beautiful food brings about respect for the process it takes to create it.

Artichokes

Artichokes are one of my favorite vegetables. Here in the Northwest, locally grown artichokes are available for just a short while each year. I usually see them on farm tables beginning in September and sometimes into October as well. Although they are grown more or less year-round in California, which supplies most supermarkets, artichokes are best in the spring and fall.

Preparing Artichokes

Wash each artichoke under cold running water. Pull off the very bottom leaves and cut off the stem, flush with the base. Try to cut it evenly so the artichoke sits upright in a serving bowl. Using scissors, snip about ¼ inch from the top of each leaf, removing the thorns. Dip the cut edges in lemon juice to preserve the color.

Use a stainless-steel or glass pot. Iron or aluminum will turn artichokes an unappetizing blue or black. For the same reason, never let aluminum foil come in contact with artichokes.

Steamed Artichokes

If it's your first time preparing artichokes, this is a great way to get started. Once you have trimmed the artichoke, fill a steamer pot with water to just below the basket and bring to a boil. Place your artichoke in the basket, set over the boiling water, lower the heat until the water is simmering, cover, and steam for about an hour. When it's done, you will be able to pull off a leaf easily. Now you can either stuff it or eat it as is. To eat the artichoke, simply hold the top part of the leaf, put the other end in your mouth, and pull off the meat with your teeth. For additional flavor, dip it in a mixture of fresh lemon juice, extra-virgin olive oil, and fresh thyme leaves.

Artichokes Stuffed with Ground Lamb and Almonds
Serves 2 to 4

Stuffed artichokes are gorgeous and fun to eat, unless you are on a date. They can be a little messy. Artichokes can be stuffed with almost anything. Here is one to get you started. Don't skimp on the stuffing.

8 ounces ground lamb
3-4 garlic cloves, minced
1 small onion, minced
1 cup lightly toasted fine fresh bread crumbs
1-2 tablespoons or so of any combination of chopped fresh herbs
      (parsley, thyme, rosemary, and oregano all go nicely with lamb)
¼ cup finely grated Parmigiano-Reggiano or Romano cheese
¼ cup coarsely ground almonds (optional)
Salt and pepper
1-2 large globe artichokes, trimmed and steamed

In a sauté pan, brown the lamb over low to medium-low heat. Pour off any fat (reserve for later use). Add the garlic and onion. Cook, stirring, for 5 minutes or so, until the garlic and onion are soft. Stir in the bread crumbs and chopped herbs.

Remove from the heat and let cool. Then add the grated cheese and almonds. Season to taste with salt and pepper.

At this point, if the filling seems dry, add the rendered fat (or a little extra-virgin olive oil). The filling should be moist, which makes it easier to stuff.

Turn the artichokes upside down and press gently but firmly into the counter. This will make the leaves open up more easily for stuffing. Place the artichokes in the bowl you are going to serve them in, then gently stuff the center and the outer leaves with filling.

Mediterranean Carrot Salad
Serves 4 to 6

This is a nice balanced mix of carrots, olives, raisins, and parsley. The vinaigrette should be tangy and just a bit fiery.

4-6 medium carrots (the farmers' markets have such a great variety of sizes and colors)
Juice and grated zest of 2 oranges
Juice and grated zest of 2 lemons
Juice and grated zest of 1 lime
¼ cup golden raisins
2 garlic cloves, minced
1 tablespoon crushed red pepper (when they're in season, a fun substitute is 1 minced Thai bird chili
     about the size of a finger)
½ cup extra-virgin olive oil
Salt and pepper
½ cup of your favorite olives, pits removed (I like green)
½ cup torn flat-leaf parsley leaves
½ cup torn mint leaves

Cut the carrots on the diagonal into slices about ½ inch thick. Usually, peeling is not necessary, and the carrots will retain more of their nutritional value if you leave the skins on. You can scrub the skins with a brush to clean. Blanch the carrots in boiling salted water for about 3 to 5 minutes. You want them still crunchy. Drain and refresh under cold water.

Place the fruit juices in a saucepan and bring to a simmer. Add the raisins, turn off the heat, and let sit until the raisins are plump, approximately 20 minutes. Add the garlic, crushed red pepper, and all the citrus zest. Whisk in the olive oil and season to taste with salt and pepper.

Toss the drained blanched carrots into the vinaigrette. Add the olives, parsley, and mint.

This is a great side dish for any meal.

Oven-Roasted Beets, Oranges, and Spring Garlic
Serves 4 to 6

Beets are a spring and fall crop, and one of the early foods that show up at my farmers' market. Green spring garlic is nestled right up against these multicolored and shapely beauties, just insisting that they be eaten together.

There are many varieties other than the deep red and golden. Chioggia, candy-striped, white, flat, and cylindrical all make for a visually exciting and delicious "first in spring" dish. I like the medium to large beets. I have to admit that baby beets (or baby anything when it comes to vegetables) just aren't that appealing to me.

I buy as many as I can carry from the farmers on market day and come home and roast them all at the same time so they are ready to go. I eat them roasted the first night with just a little olive oil, salt, and pepper. I also tear off the tops, sauté them in a bit of olive oil and chopped garlic, add fresh lemon juice to taste, and eat them alongside.

3-5 medium to large beets (about 1 pound), trimmed
1 orange, peeled and segmented
Salt and pepper
Spring Garlic Vinaigrette (page 47)
1-3 ounces bacon slices, cooked until crisp (optional)
Blue cheese, crumbled (optional)
Fresh tarragon leaves, for garnish

Preheat the oven to 350°F.

Wrap each beet tightly in aluminum foil, or place them in a covered roasting pan.

Bake for about 45 minutes. Use a skewer to pierce the beets in the center; if it slides in easily, with just a *little* resistance, they are done. Remove them from the oven and let cool in their foil jackets. When the beets are cool, remove the foil. The skins can be peeled off easily using the foil jacket or a paper towel; or wear gloves if you like, as they can stain.

Slice the beets and place in a bowl. Add the orange segments and season to taste with salt and pepper. Drizzle with some vinaigrette and toss.

Arrange on plates. Crumble crispy bacon over the top and add a bit of blue cheese for a nice salty finish! Garnish with tarragon.

Farmers' markets are about community. I see so many of the same shoppers and farmers at my market every Sunday. We have become friends. This is the best part. Next time you are at a farmers' market, begin a conversation with farmers, with people, with friends, to create a connection. This connection is what will make us better cooks, as well as more informed and more appreciative eaters. These relationships have deepened the meaning of what I do — I am a chef and I cook, every day.

How to Prepare Fava Beans

Fava beans require a few extra steps of preparation, but trust me, they are worth it. When buying fava beans, make sure they aren't too big. This is really an example of bigger is *not* better. Favas become starchy when they are too big, and they are not good. Look for smaller, greener pods.

First step is to remove the young beans from their pods. (Sounds sad, but you will quickly get over it.) You are going to need at least a few pounds of whole pods to make it worth it. Once that is done, get a big pot of boiling salted water going. Prepare an ice bath to quickly chill down your cooked beans.

Submerge your shelled beans in the boiling water for about 45 seconds to a minute. (The larger they are, the longer they will take to cook, but not much longer.) It really works well if you have a strainer that you can fill with the favas and insert directly into the boiling water. When they are cooked, submerge the favas (in the strainer) in the ice bath. Drain when chilled.

Okay, next step. Pop out each little bean from its other little jacket shell and discard the peel. Easy. Now they can be used for a salad, a pasta addition, or this tasty little appetizer, one of my favorites.

Fava Bean and Mint Croustades
Makes 18 to 20 appetizers

1 cup prepared fava beans
½ cup torn and packed fresh mint
         leaves
Salt
¼ cup extra-virgin olive oil
Grilled sliced rustic bread or crostini
Small hunk of Parmigiano-Reggiano
         or Pecorino Romano cheese

Place the fava beans in a blender
or food processor. Add the mint and
a healthy pinch or two of salt. Pulse a
few times. Gradually add the olive oil.
Taste for seasoning.

Place a nice big scoop on some grilled
bread or crostini and shave some
cheese on top. Delicious. You can also
make this simple appetizer with fresh
garden peas.

An easy way to make shaved cheese
curls is to use your potato peeler.

Spinach Salad with Wild Mushrooms and Goat Cheese
Serves 4 to 6

This is a salad I have had on my menus forever. I take it off from time to time, and end up making it anyway for my customers who can't seem to live without it.

Spinach fresh from a farmer is so delicious and tender. The bottoms of the stems can have a blush color that tells you it's fresh. You won't find that too often in a supermarket. If I have to buy it out of season for some reason, or commercially instead of direct from a farmer, I always buy organic — too many pesticides on greens, and in particular spinach, for me.

2 tablespoons extra-virgin olive oil
1 shallot, minced
1 garlic clove, minced
¼ pound fresh mushrooms, sliced (I like chanterelles, or any wild mushroom)
Large bunch of spinach leaves, cleaned and trimmed
Goat cheese, to taste
2 tablespoons chopped crispy bacon
1-2 sprigs of fresh thyme, for garnish

First prepare the vinaigrette. Set aside.

To prepare the salad, heat the olive oil in a sauté pan over medium-high heat. Add the shallot and garlic and cook until softened. Add the mushrooms and cook for about 5 minutes, or until the edges begin to brown. Remove from the heat and add the vinaigrette to the pan to warm.

To serve, mound a pile of spinach leaves on each plate. Top with a little goat cheese and the warm mushrooms and vinaigrette. Garnish with bacon and thyme.

Creamy Mustard Sherry Vinaigrette

¼ cup sherry vinegar
2 shallots, peeled
1 teaspoon mustard (I use Dijon)
1 large egg
1-1½ cups extra-virgin olive oil
Salt and pepper

Combine the vinegar, shallots, mustard, and raw egg in a blender and puree. With the motor running, slowly add the olive oil. Season to taste with salt and pepper.

Leftover vinaigrette will keep in the refrigerator for a few days.

As with nature, when it comes to food,
we don't have to re-create what it is offering
us in each season — it's a flawless design.

All vinaigrettes have the same basic building blocks. You vary the end result by changing the type of vinegar (acid) or oil you use. Whatever you use, the acid-to-oil ratio is 1 to 3. Here's a basic vinaigrette footprint.

Basic Vinaigrette
Makes 1 cup

1-2 garlic cloves, minced
1 shallot, minced
¼ cup Champagne vinegar or good-quality white wine
   vinegar
½ teaspoon Dijon mustard
¾ cup extra-virgin olive oil
Salt and pepper

In a bowl, stir together the garlic, shallot, vinegar, and mustard. Gradually whisk in the olive oil. Season to taste with salt and pepper. Store in a sealed container until ready to use.

Once you have made a basic vinaigrette, the possibilities are endless. Whether it's fruity or savory, be creative, have some fun.

Add any extra ingredients right before the olive oil or at the end for a nice bright finish, and give your whisk or blender a whirl.

During the brief two to three weeks when spring garlic shoots are available, I like to replace the minced garlic with 2 tender shoots cut into ¼-inch rings and use sherry vinegar as the acid to complement it. It's great on Oven-Roasted Beets (page 34).

Chermoula

Makes 2 to 3 cups

Many years ago, I worked with an awesome woman from Sicily. I fondly remember her with a cigarette in her mouth as she cooked over the stove. (As I said, it was a *long* time ago.) She vehemently proclaimed that the most intense and best flavors of fresh tender herbs are contained in the stem. She was absolutely correct! I often mince tender cilantro and parsley stems and sprinkle them over — well just about everything.

You are going to love this. Chermoula is a North African pesto, and it's very, very tasty. It normally contains cilantro, garlic, cumin, chilies, lemon, and olive oil, but varies from family to family. It gives dishes that extra zing.

10-12 garlic cloves, peeled
1 large pinch crushed red pepper
1 big bunch cilantro, stems and all
3 big bunches flat-leaf parsley, stems and all
4 tablespoons cumin seeds, toasted and ground (optional) (see note)
1 teaspoon hot smoked paprika
6 tablespoons lemon juice and the grated zest
2 teaspoons salt
1½ cups extra-virgin olive oil (approximately)

In a food processor, chop the garlic first. Then add everything else except the oil. Blend. You want this chunky. With the motor running, gradually add olive oil until you have a loose, pesto-like paste.

Note: Cumin adds a nice flavor. I recommend taking the time to toast it in a sauté pan for a few minutes and then grinding it. Go ahead and toast a few ounces extra, then store in a sealed container in the fridge to use later when you don't have the time.

Tomatoes

When the markets are loaded with tomatoes, I try to take advantage of the opportunity. Plum tomatoes make the best sauce. This is the exact way that good-quality canned tomatoes are made. They are picked when they are ripe and ready, and then they are canned. It is always better to use canned plum or Roma tomatoes in the off-season rather than the tasteless "fresh" tomatoes that are available commercially. Here's how I hold them over for winter and a few ways to enjoy them at their peak.

Herb-Roasted Tomatoes

1 pound plum tomatoes, cut in half lengthwise
Extra-virgin olive oil
5-8 garlic cloves, crushed and peeled
Ample sprigs of thyme, sage, and rosemary
Salt and pepper
1-2 tablespoons balsamic vinegar

Preheat the oven to 450°F.

Place the tomatoes cut side up on a sheet pan. Drizzle olive oil all over the tomatoes. Add the garlic and herbs. Season to taste with salt and pepper. Roast for 20 minutes, or until they are tender but still retain their shape.

Drizzle vinegar over the roasted tomatoes. Refrigerate until chilled. Use or freeze for later use.

I usually grab all the plum tomatoes I can find throughout the season and prepare them this way. After cooling them in the refrigerator, I pack the entire concoction in ziplock bags and toss them in the freezer. These tasty tomatoes find their way into my pasta dishes, pizza toppings, soups, and sauces.

Love these little dumplings. I have a hard time calling them gnocchi. I can think of one Italian teacher of mine who would cringe if I did! These *pillows of love* (as one of my friends calls them) are a fine treat in the summertime when I don't want to take the time to make the traditional potato gnocchi. They are quick and super easy. A fresh heirloom tomato sauce that requires no more than a grater, a little garlic, and some fresh herbs is a perfect accompaniment.

Ricotta Dumplings with Peas, Pancetta, and Tomatoes
Serves 4 to 6

1 pound fresh ricotta, drained
1 large egg
½ cup freshly grated Parmigiano-Reggiano cheese
½ teaspoon salt
Pinch of freshly grated nutmeg
1 cup all-purpose flour, divided, plus more for dusting

In a bowl, gently stir together the ricotta, egg, cheese, salt, and nutmeg. Add ¾ cup of the flour and mix with a wooden spoon just until blended, being careful not to overhandle it. If the dough is too sticky, add a little more flour. Chill the dough for 30 minutes.

Spread the remaining ¼ cup of flour onto your board or countertop. Place the dough on top and roll gently into a long, thick log. Cut the log into 4 pieces. Adding a little more flour each time, roll the 4 smaller logs into ropes about ½ inch in diameter. Cut the ropes into 1-inch lengths. Place the dumplings on a sheet pan dusted with flour. Be careful that they don't touch each other.

2 tablespoons extra-virgin olive oil
3 garlic cloves, minced or sliced
½ cup chopped shallots
4-6 slices pancetta (or bacon, cut into ¼-inch dice and sautéed until crisp)
1 tablespoon balsamic vinegar
1 cup dry white wine
4 medium tomatoes, diced
2-3 sprigs freshly picked thyme, leaves removed and chopped
1 cup blanched fresh shelled peas or snap peas cut on the diagonal into ¼- to ½-inch slices

Fresh herbs
Extra-virgin olive oil (optional)
Freshly grated Parmigiano-Reggiano cheese

To prepare the sauce, heat the olive oil in a large sauté pan over low heat. Add the garlic and shallots and cook until caramelized. Add the pancetta and sauté for 2 minutes. With a slotted spoon, remove the pancetta from the pan and set aside.

Add the vinegar, wine, tomatoes, and thyme leaves to the remaining oil in the sauté pan. Cook until reduced by half. Add the peas and half of the crisped pancetta, and heat until warmed through. Set aside and keep warm.

Bring a pot of salted water to a gentle boil. Lower the heat. Working in small batches, gently add the dumplings. When they float to the top, they're ready. Lift them out of the water with a slotted spoon and gently add to the warm sauce.

To serve, spoon the dumplings and sauce onto warm plates. Scatter a small handful of fresh herbs over the dumplings. Drizzle a little olive oil over each serving, then sprinkle with grated Parmigiano-Reggiano and crisped pancetta. Serve immediately.

I always test my dumplings before I commit to cooking all of them. Cut and drop a few dumplings into the boiling water. If the dough is too loose, the dumplings will disintegrate in the water. If this happens, I just add enough flour to the remaining dough to bind them a bit more.

Five-Minute Fresh Garden Tomato and Herb Sauce
Makes about 1½ cups

1 pound heirloom tomatoes
Fresh garlic clove(s)
Extra-virgin olive oil
1 tablespoon balsamic vinegar
Fresh tender herbs such as basil, chervil, tarragon, mint, oregano – any
      combination will be spectacular if fresh and recently harvested
Salt and pepper

Grate your perfect farmers' market tomatoes into a bowl. Toss the leftover skin away. If some skin gets into the sauce, that's totally okay. What could be bad about that?

Grate a piece of fresh garlic (or more if you like) right into the tomatoes. Add a generous pour of your favorite olive oil and the vinegar. Tear up a handful or so of your herbs and toss them into the sauce. Reserve a bit of the fresh herbs for garnish. Season to taste with salt and pepper.

This is a simple, fresh-tasting sauce that goes great with a fillet of Herb-Crusted Fish (page 60) or a plate of Ricotta Dumplings (page 56).

Herb-Crusted Fish with Garden Tomato Sauce and Summer Vegetables

Serves 1

4-5 ounces skinless fillet of white fish such as halibut or black cod (salmon is good, too)
1 tablespoon extra-virgin olive oil, plus more for brushing and drizzling
Salt and pepper
Handful of a variety of fresh herbs, finely chopped
1 teaspoon butter (optional)
Five-Minute Fresh Garden Tomato and Herb Sauce (page 59)
English peas and fresh green beans, lightly sautéed
Fresh lemon juice

Brush the fish with a little olive oil. Season with salt and pepper.

Spread the chopped herbs on a plate. Lay the fish on top, gently pressing into the herbs. Turn the fish over.

Heat a sauté skillet over medium-high heat until it's good and hot, and then add the tablespoon of olive oil to the pan. Add the butter for extra flavor if you'd like. Since the pan is already hot, the oil needs just a second or two to catch up. (That's the secret to good searing technique — heat up the pan first.)

Gently lay the fish herb-side down in the hot pan. Lower the heat to medium and sear for 3 to 5 minutes. The herbs will be a blackish-green color and crispy. Flip the fish with a metal spatula. Since most of the cooking was done on the first side, the fish will be cooked in just another minute or two, depending on its thickness.

Spoon some tomato sauce, either warm or room temperature, onto a serving plate and place your fish in the middle. Scatter the sautéed peas and green beans around the fish. Drizzle a bit of olive oil and fresh lemon juice over the fish.

Vine-Ripened Tomatoes with Browned Sage Butter and Parmesan Curls

This is another great way to enjoy a stack of sliced vine-ripened tomatoes. Serve with a crusty slice of bread.

Vine-ripened tomatoes, preferably more than one variety
Salt and pepper
Browned Sage Butter
Parmigiano-Reggiano, Pecorino Romano, or your favorite cheese

Slice the tomatoes. Season on all sides with a little salt and pepper. Lay them overlapping on a plate or platter.

Pour a little Browned Sage Butter over the tomatoes. With a vegetable peeler, shave off curls of cheese over the top. Use any cheese you like — it really doesn't matter as long as *you* like the cheese. This dish is great with a soft goat cheese as well.

Browned Sage Butter

3 tablespoons unsalted butter
1 tablespoon chopped fresh sage
1 teaspoon fresh lemon juice
Dash of salt

Heat a large sauté pan over low heat. Add the butter and cook until very brown and bubbly, about 3 minutes. Add the sage. Remove from the heat. Stir in the lemon juice. Season with salt.

Catalan Tomato Bread

Serves 4 to 6

1 baguette
1-2 heads of garlic
Extra-virgin olive oil
2 ripe tomatoes
Browned Sage Butter
Manchego, Pecorino Romano, or your favorite cheese (optional)

Preheat the oven to 300°F.

Slice the baguette on the bias into approximately 1-inch-thick slices.

Separate the garlic cloves, peel, and crush. Rub the garlic over the bread slices.

Place the bread slices on a baking sheet. Drizzle with a little olive oil. Toast in the oven for about 10 minutes, or until the bread is just a little crunchy. Alternatively, place the slices on a grill and toast slightly.

Cut the tomatoes into ¼- to ½-inch dice. Place them on the "croustades" and pour the Browned Sage Butter over the tomatoes. Garnish with cheese or no cheese! Up to you.

The Spanish have a peasant appetizer they call tomato bread. It's usually a slice of baguette rubbed with garlic and then grilled. The bread is then topped with crushed tomato and olive oil. It's really simple and delicious. That was the inspiration for this dish.

Mediterranean Tomato and Bread Salad
Serves 4 to 6

Heirloom tomatoes are so abundant in the summer. Experiment with the different varieties. Mix the colors and celebrate tomatoes!

Approximately ½ baguette, cut into 1½-inch cubes
Approximately 2 tablespoons extra-virgin olive oil (see note)
Salt and pepper (optional)

3 medium fresh tomatoes
½ cup of your favorite olives, drained
¼ red onion, thinly sliced
4 tablespoons extra-virgin olive oil
Juice and grated zest of 1 lemon
Salt and pepper
Flat-leaf parsley leaves
1 bunch purslane, if available (optional)
½ cup feta cheese chunks, preferably cut from a bulk chunk
2 tablespoons slivered almonds or pine nuts, toasted (optional)

To prepare the croutons, combine the bread cubes, olive oil, and salt and pepper to taste. Spread on a rimmed baking sheet and bake in a 325°F oven for 5 to 10 minutes, or toast in a pan on the stovetop. The key to good croutons is a crispy exterior and a chewy, soft interior. You have to watch them whether you toast them in the oven or on the stovetop. Don't let them get too hard. In a bread salad, you want them to absorb the juices from the salad. Set the croutons aside and let cool.

Slice the tomatoes into wedges or nice bite-size chunks. Place in a salad bowl with the olives and red onion. Add the olive oil and the lemon juice and zest. Season to taste with salt and pepper. Add the croutons, some of the parsley leaves, and the purslane. Toss. Taste. Add more lemon juice if you like.

Arrange the salad on a platter and top with chunks of feta, almonds, and parsley leaves.
Serve immediately.

Note: For an optional twist on the croutons, crush a clove or two of garlic into the olive oil and warm it on the stove before drizzling over the cubed bread for toasting.

In the summer when we are outside and active, we have full-flavored tomatoes that we can just slice and go.

English Pea and Mint Soup
Serves 6 to 8

2 tablespoons extra-virgin olive oil
1 white onion, chopped
4 cups vegetable stock
3 cups freshly shelled garden peas
1 cup fresh spinach leaves or watercress
Grated zest of 1 lemon
Handful of mint leaves
1 cup crème fraîche or sour cream
1 tablespoon unsalted butter
Salt and pepper

Heat the olive oil in a soup pot over medium-high heat. Add the onion and sauté until soft. Add the vegetable stock and bring to a boil. Add the peas and cook for about 3 minutes, or until tender. Remove from the heat and let cool for a few minutes.

Working in batches, ladle some of the mixture into a blender, filling about halfway. Add a small handful of spinach or watercress and some of the lemon zest and mint leaves. This gives it even more flavor and helps to keep it a fresh green color. Blend thoroughly. With the motor running, add some crème fraîche and a bit of butter. Blend until smooth. Repeat the process until all the soup is made. Season to taste with salt and pepper.

Keep the soup warm in a pot and reheat gently when you're ready to eat. Garnish with Pea, Mint, and Basil Pistou.

Pea, Mint, and Basil Pistou

Crush a handful of peas, then add lots of chopped fresh mint and basil and some olive oil to create a chunky relish. Add salt and pepper to taste. Put a dollop on each serving of soup.

Sea Scallops with Spiced Orange Vinaigrette and Fruited Couscous

Serves 1

4 ounces sea scallops
3 tablespoons cumin seeds, toasted
Salt and pepper
1 tablespoon extra-virgin olive oil, or more as needed
1 teaspoon unsalted butter
Fruited Couscous (page 72)
Torn mint and cilantro leaves, for garnish
Spiced Orange Vinaigrette (page 137)

Remove the muscle on the side of each scallop. It can be pulled off easily with your fingers. Lay the scallops on paper towels and pat dry.

With a spice grinder or mortar and pestle, coarsely grind the freshly toasted cumin seeds. Place the ground cumin in a bowl.

Season the scallops with salt and pepper to taste. Crust the flat sides of each scallop by gently pressing into the ground cumin.

In a large sauté pan, heat 1 tablespoon or so of olive oil and the butter over medium heat. When the butter begins to brown, gently place each scallop in the sizzling butter. Leave the scallops undisturbed for about 2 to 3 minutes to get nice and brown on one side. Then flip the scallops and cook for another 1 to 2 minutes, turning off the heat under the pan after a minute or so. This will give you medium-rare scallops. Be careful not to overcook them.

Spoon some couscous onto your plate and arrange the scallops over and around it. Garnish with mint and cilantro, and a drizzle of vinaigrette.

This recipe is best with larger scallops. I like Alaskan weathervanes.

I really like couscous. It's simple and quick to cook, and very fresh-tasting. I like it plain, with just a little butter and fresh herbs. I also like it dressed up. This is the dressed-up version.

Note: Dried apricots, figs, and dates are good; currants, dried cherries, or golden raisins are wonderful additions. Any combination of two or more of the fruits is fine as long as it suits you. You want to use about a cup of dried fruit for about a cup of dry couscous. Remember, the grain will expand two to three times.

Fruited Couscous
Serves 4

½ cup slivered almonds
Extra-virgin olive oil
1 red onion, diced
1¾ cups (total) fresh orange juice with a generous squeeze of fresh lemon juice (see note)
1 cup dry couscous (small grain)
1 cup dried fruit, chopped if large (see note)
2 tablespoons unsalted butter
Grated zest of 1 orange and 1 lemon
Salt and pepper
1 cup or more chopped fresh herbs, e.g., cilantro, basil, tarragon, or mint
A pinch or two of crushed red pepper

Lightly toast the almonds in a small sauté pan over low heat on the stovetop or in the oven. Set aside.

Put a glug of olive oil in a preheated sauté pan over low heat. When hot, add the onion and cook, stirring, until soft.

Place the juice in a saucepan and bring to a boil.

Put the couscous in a mixing bowl (remember, the grain will more than double in volume). Add the dried fruit and sautéed onion. Pour the boiling liquid over the couscous mixture, which should be enough to cover by ½ inch or so. Stir and then cover tightly with plastic wrap to steam for about 30 minutes.

Remove the plastic wrap from the bowl. Add the butter and the zests, and lightly fluff with a fork. Season to taste with salt and pepper.

Now is when you add the crunch. Stir in the toasted almonds and your chopped fresh herbs. I also like a pinch or two of red pepper for a zip. Be sure to retaste and then reseason with salt and pepper if needed.

Eat this couscous at room temperature, with chicken, lamb, or fish. It's also delicious all by itself. If the finished quantity is too much for one meal, it'll still taste great the next day or two.

Note: You can use vegetable or chicken broth instead of the orange/lemon combination, though the citrus juices add a nice twist. Experiment and find your favorite combination.

Anything that is good eaten raw can be added after the couscous is cooked. Use your eyes and senses to figure out what and how much. Optional ingredients such as chopped fresh tomatoes, different varieties of toasted nuts, peeled and chopped oranges, and even pitted olives are great additions. In the summer, when sweet Sun Gold cherry tomatoes are at the peak of their season, add 1½ cups or so, sliced, to boost color and flavor.

Clams and mussels are perfect for family-style meals and easy to prepare.

Skillet-Roasted Clams and Mussels

Serves 4 to 6 as an appetizer, or 2 to 3 as an entrée

2 tablespoons extra-virgin olive oil, plus more for drizzling
½ pound fresh chorizo or hot Italian sausage (see note)
4 garlic cloves, crushed
2 whole shallots, sliced thin
1 cup canned crushed tomatoes
A healthy pinch of crushed red pepper
1 pound Manila clams
½ cup dry white wine, water, or stock
1 pound mussels, debearded
Juice of 1 lemon, plus lemon wedges for garnish
Fresh parsley and cilantro leaves, for garnish
Crusty bread, for serving

To clean the mussels, grab the bearded part and pull down gently to remove it. Give both the clams and mussels a good rinse.

In a 10-inch sauté pan or cast-iron skillet, heat olive oil over medium heat. Add the sausage and cook until nicely browned, stirring to crumble.

Stir in the garlic, shallots, tomatoes, and red pepper. Cook for 5 minutes or so, then add the clams. Add the wine, cover, and cook for 5 to 10 minutes, depending on their size, then add the mussels. Once the shellfish have opened, finish with a squeeze of fresh lemon.

I like using the cast-iron skillet as my serving dish. Scatter parsley and cilantro leaves over the top. Drizzle with some really nice olive oil and add lemon wedges for garnish. Don't forget the bread to sop up the juices!

Note: Of course you can omit the sausage if you are vegetarian, but don't if you enjoy pork! It's an incredible combination.

Cider-Steamed Clams with Apple Relish and Chorizo
Serves 4 as an entreé, or 6 as an appetizer

½ pound fresh chorizo or your favorite sausage, either bulk or squeezed out of the casings
2 pounds clams, rinsed
2 cups Washington dry cider (or white wine if none is available)
Juice and grated zest of 1 lemon
A few garlic cloves, sliced
A few shallots, sliced
Crusty bread, for serving

In a pot, brown the chorizo over medium heat, stirring to break up the meat.

Add the clams, dry cider, lemon juice and zest, garlic, and shallots to the pot. Cover and let steam over medium-high heat until the clams open.

Place the steamed clams in a serving bowl with some of the broth. Serve with Apple Relish and a crusty loaf of bread for sopping up the juices.

Apple Relish

3 Washington-grown apples, cored and diced – approximately 2½ to 3 cups (see note)
2 fresh roasted poblano chiles (page 221), skinned, seeded, and chopped
½ cup golden raisins
¼ cup fresh lime juice and the grated zest
1 tablespoon brown sugar
¾ teaspoon hot smoked paprika
½ bunch fresh cilantro, chopped
½ teaspoon salt, or to taste

Place the diced apples in a bowl and mix with the other ingredients.

This is also a good little relish for chicken and pork.

Note: Washington is apple country. A few of my favorite varieties are Jonagold, Pink Lady, and Braeburn. All have a nice balance. I would choose any apple, however, that was fresh and local.

Building community and sharing our food is not about creating the perfect plate, but about sourcing, working, and discovering or rediscovering the perfect foods. And with that understanding comes the real joy of cooking and preparing meals for ourselves, our family, and others. This uncovering process will bring us into a *whole* new relationship with our planet and each other.

My experiences with farmers have led me to a relationship with the food I eat and cook that I never had before. It began with one of my first farms, where the farmers raised mostly vegetables, a few chickens, and a pig or two. They were at many of the farmers' markets on a weekly basis, and I bought from them for one of my restaurants. Over time we formed a relationship that ultimately raised my awareness. My journey has been purposeful in opening my eyes to the pleasures of unconditional giving, which is the gift we have received from our planet.

Today, that unconditional giving on our part has been altered. Our planet needs some crucial nurturing. We can give it the nurturing it deserves by supporting our tenders, our local farmers, our farmers' markets, our chefs, our communities. I hope you will be inspired to sometimes buy in bulk a product that is abundant and easily dried, canned, or frozen for later use. Whether you make a commitment to go all the way with this idea, or do it only from time to time, it makes a difference. Perhaps those farmers will be encouraged to keep growing because they have found a loyal customer. Every day in my choices, I am looking at how I can support my community, my neighborhood — they are family.

On Communal Foods and Paella

I couldn't dream of creating a book that didn't include my thoughts on paella and a recipe or two. I enjoy dishes that bring people together in a food-friendly way. If you are looking for a different sort of one-pot meal, paella can be a really good choice. It's an easy dish to make, delicious and impressive.

Once you understand the basic concept behind paella, the variations are endless. Now, of course if you happen to be from Spain, you probably just slammed this book shut! There are as many paella recipes as there are Spaniards. Understand that all regions have their own versions and are adamant that theirs is the best and most authentic. It is the same for the French and their cassoulet, Latinos and posole, Italians and pizza. The truth is that the most authentic dishes are often considered peasant food. These dishes develop from the resources available, period. They come from the passionate soul of a cook who cares to create something meaningful and sustaining from the abundance of the land and the sea.

In America, getting us to take the time to actually cook anything that requires more than a shake of the bag or tap of the microwave button is a monumental accomplishment.

Whether you use chicken, sausage, peas, artichokes, tomatoes, clams or mussels, or any combination (or all) of these ingredients is completely up to you. The only sacrilegious addition to the King of Rice Dishes would be cheese. Simply, don't do it. It's not risotto — just ask an Italian!

I first encountered traditional paella in small towns along the coast of Spain. This is a true community event, one that speaks to the value and importance of communal eating. These coastal towns rely heavily on the fishing industry for their livelihood. There is a good bit of agriculture as well. All of these fishermen and farmers take their catch and daily harvest to market every day. What doesn't sell ends up in a huge communal paella pan in the central square of the village. That's how the poultry, vegetables, and shellfish (classic combination) ended up in the pan. It sits over a large wood-burning pit. It's fabulous to look at and be a part of. The big hit with the kids (and adults) is the rice that sticks to the pan after all the cooking is done and most of the eating.

Paella's humble beginnings teach us important lessons in community, economics, relationships, and sustainability. One of the true messages of paella is this: make enough for the village, use it all, know where it comes from, and use what is available. It's all good.

Using a traditional paella pan with handles on the side is fun and authentic. These pans come in a few different sizes, depending on how many people you are serving. Paella can be made on top of your stove or on a barbecue or even over a campfire. (I like to go camping. I make this every time and have no trouble getting friends to come along.)

Home-Style Paella Valenciana
Serves 4 to 6

Depending on where you live, this can be an expensive dish to make. These amounts are general guidelines and can be more or less, so vary it according to what's available at your store, seasonal items like fresh tender green beans, or budget. Remember that the more ingredients you use, the less of each you will need.

¾-1½ cups fresh chorizo or other flavorful sausage such as hot Italian (I like
        a couple ounces per person)
Extra-virgin olive oil (optional)
½ cup sliced onions or shallots
A few garlic cloves, crushed
½ cup canned crushed tomatoes
1 cup white rice – Arborio (rinse before using), jasmine, or paella rice
Tiny pinch of saffron, rehydrated in a teaspoon of water
Water

Place the paella pan over medium heat. (If you don't have a paella pan, use an 8- to 10-inch ovenproof sauté pan or cast-iron skillet.) Add the chorizo to the pan and brown for a few minutes, breaking up with the back of a spoon. (A splash of olive oil may be needed to prevent sticking, depending on how fatty your sausage is.)

Add the onions and garlic and cook until caramelized. Add the tomatoes, rice, and saffron and stir to blend. Add 1½ cups of water and cook slowly, uncovered, over medium heat. If the liquid is close to evaporating and the rice is still crunchy, add water ¼ cup at a time until it is done. When most of the liquid has evaporated and the rice is just al dente, remove the pan from the heat and set aside.

The treatment of the shellfish and chicken is not traditional, but making it this way will keep the paella from getting too dry and the seafood from being overcooked.

Extra-virgin olive oil
4 garlic cloves, crushed
12 mussels
12 clams
12 large shrimp

You could also add calamari.

2-4 ounces cooked chicken per person

Pinch of crushed red pepper
1 cup dry white wine
¼ cup canned crushed tomatoes
A handful of cooked vegetables such as green beans (cut into 2-inch lengths),
    snap peas, green peas, etc.
Dash of fresh lemon juice
Salt and pepper
2-3 scallions, slivered, for garnish
3 tablespoons chopped fresh flat-leaf parsley and/or cilantro, for garnish
Lemon wedges, for garnish

Preheat the oven to 350°F.

Heat a large sauté pan over low heat, add a bit of olive oil, and sauté the garlic until lightly browned. Add the shellfish, chicken, and crushed red pepper. Stir in the wine and tomatoes. Raise the heat to medium-low, cover, and cook for 3 to 4 minutes, or just until the shellfish barely open. Add the cooked veggies, lemon juice, and salt and pepper to taste.

Arrange the chicken and seafood mixture atop the prepared rice, then heat in the oven for about 10 minutes, or until everything is nice and hot.

Scatter slivered scallions and parsley and/or cilantro over the top. Add a few lemon wedges as well. Serve immediately.

When you roast a whole chicken and haven't eaten it all, this paella is a great way to use some of it up. If you don't have enough leftovers, you can also roast some breasts and thighs rubbed with Chimichurri (page 147) in the oven ahead of time. Then simply pull the meat off the bone in large bite-size pieces or leave the pieces whole, as long as they are a manageable size for serving.

I started reading, I started to pay attention, talking to my farmer friends, to my chef friends differently — wanting to understand more. That was probably the most significant part of my journey — things that I thought I knew but really didn't.

Pork Ribs

The method that you use to make successful ribs is just as important as the ingredients you use. Many of us have our favorite rub for meats. My suggestion is to rub the ribs with your preferred spice rub — or mine — and let them sit in the refrigerator overnight.

Preheat the oven to 225°F.

Wrap your seasoned ribs in foil, or place them in a covered roasting pan, and roast them low and slow for about two hours. The meat should be fork tender. At this point you can either continue finishing them in the oven or remove the foil and move them to a low-heat grill, both for about another 40 minutes.

While they're finishing on the grill, if you want to add BBQ sauce, now is the time to do it. Baste them with your sauce every 15 minutes, turning from time to time to let the ribs become a bit caramelized. They'll get nicely browned and sticky looking, with the meat almost falling off the bone. To finish them in the oven, after 25 minutes remove the foil and brush with BBQ sauce. Return to the oven for 15 more minutes.

If you have wood chips, soak them the night before and toss them on the barbecue for about the last 15 minutes to give the ribs some smoke flavor.

Serve with Roasted Farmers' Market Corn with Herbed Chili Butter (page 232) and Vine-Ripened Tomatoes with Browned Sage Butter (page 62).

Tamara's Pork Rib Rub

Makes 1½ to 2 cups, enough for about 3 to 4 racks

I like ribs vinegary and smoky — not saucy, usually. I actually like my sauce on the side. That's the Carolina girl in me.

But if I *were* to use a sauce, I have this:

1 cup light or dark brown sugar
¼ cup granulated sugar
2 tablespoons sweet paprika
1 tablespoon salt
1 tablespoon ground cumin
1 tablespoon cayenne pepper
1 teaspoon ground cinnamon
1 teaspoon ground allspice
¼ cup red wine vinegar or any other kind on hand

Combine all the ingredients in a bowl and mix well.

Cuban BBQ Sauce

Makes about 4 cups

2 tablespoons ancho chile powder
2 teaspoons sweet paprika
2 teaspoons ground cumin
½ teaspoon cayenne pepper
1½ tablespoons extra-virgin olive oil
½ cup tomato puree
1 cup fresh orange juice and the grated zest
½ cup strong espresso, freshly brewed
½ cup red wine vinegar
2 teaspoons freshly cracked pepper
3 tablespoons molasses
5 garlic cloves, minced
Salt to taste

Combine all the ingredients and stir to mix well. Baste the ribs with the sauce while they are finishing on the grill or in the oven. To serve this sauce on the side, simmer for 15 to 20 minutes over low heat to thicken a bit.

As a chef,
I began to look
more closely at
why I wanted
to support my
farmers' markets
and local farms.
The excellent
flavor of the
meats, fruits, and
vegetables was
my primary
reason — in
the beginning.
Ultimately, it
has led me on
a journey about
relationships,
and about being
connected.

Roast Pig
Serves 6 to 8

This is my signature dish.

1 pork shoulder, boneless or bone-in, from 3 to 5 pounds
Extra-virgin olive oil
Salt and pepper
2 cups dry white wine, such as sauvignon blanc
2 cups chicken stock
1 bay leaf (optional)
Sprig of fresh thyme
1 large carrot, diced
2 celery ribs, diced
4 garlic cloves, crushed
Crusty bread, for serving

SAUCE
Extra-virgin olive oil
3 shallots, sliced
4-6 garlic cloves, minced
1 pound bulk fresh chorizo sausage
1 teaspoon hot smoked paprika
1 pound clams
1 cup dry white wine
3 cups broth from braising the pork
Juice and grated zest of 1 lemon
Salt and pepper

There's nothing like the taste of fresh authentic smoked paprika. If hot smoked paprika is not available, you can add a pinch of cayenne pepper to the smoked paprika as a substitute.

Preheat the oven to 300°F.

Rub the pork with olive oil and season with salt and pepper. Heat a large pot on the stovetop over medium-high heat. Add the pork and sear until browned, about 3 minutes per side. Add the wine, stock, herbs, carrot, celery, and garlic. Braise, uncovered, in the oven for about 3 to 4 hours. Midway through, rotate the pork, turning the top side down into the liquid, and cover for the remaining time. When the pork is falling off the bone or fork-tender, remove it to a plate and set aside to cool.

Strain the juices from the pot. You will have about 2 to 3 cups. You can discard the vegetables, or for a slightly thicker and tastier sauce, press them through a sieve and add to the pan juices.

When it is cool enough to handle, pull serving-size chunks from the pork shoulder. Set aside.

At this point you can refrigerate the pork overnight to resume cooking the next day if you choose.

To prepare the sauce, wipe out the pot (no need to wash). Heat a splash of olive oil over medium heat. Add the shallots and garlic and sauté until soft. Add the chorizo and brown, stirring to crumble.

Add the pork pieces, paprika, clams, wine, and the pork broth. It may be necessary to add a little water if you don't have the full 3 cups of broth. Simmer, uncovered, for about 10 minutes. If the clams open, quickly remove them and let the liquid continue to reduce. This should be not too soupy but not too thick (you want sauce for the bread!).

Return the clams to the pot along with the lemon juice and zest. Check for salt and pepper.

Place the pork and clams in the middle of your serving dish and pour all the goodness over the pork. Serve with crusty bread.

I garnish mine with pickled onions.

Braised Beef Shanks
Serves 4 to 6

Parchment paper
Butter
2 beef shanks, cut 2 inches thick into approximately
    6 pieces
Salt and pepper
Extra-virgin olive oil
2 medium carrots, diced
1 large onion, diced
4 garlic cloves, minced
1 celery rib, diced
½ cup red wine vinegar
1 cup chopped canned tomatoes
2 tablespoons tomato puree
2 cups dry red wine (remember, always cook with
    wine that is drinkable)
4 cups beef broth, or enough to cover the shanks by
    a couple of inches
A few thyme (or rosemary) sprigs
Freshly chopped parsley, for garnish

Preheat the oven to 300°F. Cut a piece of parchment paper the size of your roasting pan (it's best to use a pan that the shanks fit into snugly). Melt some butter and brush it on the parchment with a pastry brush; set aside.

Season the shanks really well with salt and pepper. Get your large roasting pan (or you can do this in batches in a sauté pan), add a few glugs of olive oil, and let it get hot on the stovetop (but not smoking hot) over medium to medium-high heat. Add the seasoned shanks and sear on all sides to seal in the juices. This will also give your sauce a nice brown color. After the shanks are well browned on all sides, remove them from the pan.

Add the carrots, onion, garlic, and celery to the pan, and sauté for a few minutes. Add the vinegar, tomatoes, and tomato puree. Stir and cook for about 5 minutes. Add the wine, beef broth, thyme, and the seared shanks. Lay the parchment paper, buttered side down, over the shanks. Cover the roasting pan with foil and place it in the oven. (Using both parchment and foil will keep the meat nice and moist. The foil seals the moisture in the pan, and the buttered parchment directly on top of the meat mixture acts as a form of self-basting.)

In a couple of hours, the shanks should be done. The meat will just begin to pull away from the bone. Remove the shanks from the pan. If the sauce is thin, simmer the liquid and vegetables on the stovetop over medium to medium-low heat until you have a nice thick sauce. Be sure to scrape the bottom of the pan — you don't want to leave any of that behind! Season to taste.

Garnish with parsley and serve with Vine-Ripened Tomatoes with Browned Sage Butter (page 62), Smashed Potatoes (page 243), and Tender Herb and Wild Greens Relish. This dish is delicious with risotto as well.

Tender Herb and Wild Greens Relish

I learned how to make this years and years ago from the first Italian chef I worked for. It's very tasty and easy. In the summer, my own garden overflows with herbs and wild greens. Sometimes I have too many at the restaurants as well, and this will take care of them.

I use this relish as a garnish on soups, sandwiches, fish, and meat. It's very versatile and uses all those tender herbs! I usually leave rosemary, thyme, and sage out of the mix because they tend to be a bit toothsome.

Quantities and varieties are up to you. Just experiment. Always look for balance. If you make this and all you taste is tarragon, then you should add some other herbs. When adding vinegar, put in just a drop or two and watch how the acid brightens the herb mixture without it tasting like vinegar. If it tastes like vinegar, then oops, too much vinegar — add more herbs or greens. The herbs on this list are really nice in any combination.

Tarragon
Basil
Parsley
Mint
Oregano
Cilantro
Arugula
Wild greens, tender chard, and spring garlic are wonderful additions
Vinegar — champagne, rice, or white wine
Lots of slivered garlic
Grated lemon zest
Extra-virgin olive oil
Salt

Cut or tear the herbs and greens into thin strips or pieces, to achieve roughly the same size. Place in a bowl and add a splash of vinegar, garlic, lemon zest, and a generous drizzle of olive oil, getting it wet enough to bind it like a pesto. Season to taste with salt.

Pack the relish in a mason jar with olive oil to cover. Store in the fridge. You can use it immediately, but the longer it sits, the more the flavors meld. Whenever you remove some relish from the jar, be sure that what's left is covered with olive oil, adding more if necessary.

Even though it might get a little brown, the relish will last for a couple of weeks. Or to save a little summer freshness for the winter, halfway fill ziplock bags, seal, and pop them in the freezer. Use for sauces, vinaigrettes, marinades — there are endless opportunities for your herb relish!

We must always keep in mind that farms are disappearing at an alarming rate. Once that farmland is gone, never again will that land produce food. Food is a product that comes from the earth. We need our local farmers in order to enjoy our craft and for you to enjoy your meals, period!

I grill in the winter as well as the summer. Roasts are so easy, and they really take on a different flavor when you cook them on the grill. I think we often stay away from meat cuts such as roasts in the summer because we feel that they are more appropriate for the winter. But I have found that I enjoy these slow-cooked meats in the summer as well. Big, thick slices of ripe tomatoes with Browned Sage Butter (page 62) and a roast on the barbecue — nothing better. It's fun to take a look at how we are used to doing things and then create new eating experiences by simply adding unexpected ideas.

Roast Boneless Lamb Shoulder
Serves 6 to 8 (with leftovers)

Moroccan Spice Rub
3-5 pounds boneless lamb shoulder
Extra-virgin olive oil

Massage a few tablespoons of the spice rub into the meat, and then let the seasoned meat sit out for 10 to 20 minutes to get to room temperature. Just before cooking, drizzle some olive oil all over the seasoned meat.

Preheat the grill or preheat the oven to 300°F.

First sear the seasoned shoulder on all sides and get the meat nice and brown. Do this on the hot grill or in a hot pan on top of the stove if you're going to oven-roast.

Then turn your grill down to a low setting and close the lid. Check the meat every 30 minutes, turning it over to ensure even browning. It will take about 2 hours.

If you are using the oven, roast the meat for about the same amount of time.

Either way, you want your meat to be medium, which is about 135 to 140°F at the center of the roast, but be sure to remove it from the heat at about 120 to 125°F and it will coast the rest of the way.

Serve with Fruited Couscous (page 72) and a bowl of Chermoula (page 48) for a tasty condiment.

Moroccan Spice Rub

This is a delicious rub for lamb and poultry. It will keep in a tightly sealed jar in a cool, dark place for several months, so make plenty to have on hand.

5 bay leaves
1 tablespoon dried thyme
1 tablespoon white or black
    peppercorns
½ teaspoon ground mace (optional)
1 tablespoon ground nutmeg –
    grated fresh from a whole
    nutmeg is best
1 tablespoon whole cloves
1 tablespoon ground cinnamon

In a spice mill, grind all the ingredients until powdered, about 1 minute. Store in a tightly sealed jar.

Mace is from the outer sheath of the nutmeg. It's similar in aroma and flavor, but adds another layer of complexity.

Economics, kids on different schedules, little time left in the day to make home-cooked meals — this is the reality of our busy lives. I hope these recipes will demystify cooking and generate an understanding of how to prepare food simply and in most cases quickly. The best way to do this is first to learn how to cook a given vegetable, fruit, grain, meat, or fish in the simplest and most straightforward way. Eating and knowing how to prepare a variety of foods is the key to becoming a great cook. Once the fear of a particular vegetable or grain or any other ingredient is gone, the process of combining this food with that herb, and that with this, becomes fun, creative, and healthy.

Remember that perfect foods — fruits and vegetables — come out of the ground and not out of a box or can. If you think you don't know how to cook, start with good ingredients and have on hand a little olive oil, salt, and pepper — and you are on your way! The thing about cooking and planning is that you need to play; it is really fun to think about where foods come from, who their neighbors are. Food that grows together goes together.

Whole Roasted Fish
Serves 4 to 6

Some food items don't really need a recipe. You just feel
your way through it. It can be intimidating at first. Then
you do it, and you realize it's not too hard and you will
have a better idea next time what to expect. Cooking
is not an exact science. So don't get too caught up in
a recipe all the time.

Almost any fish can be roasted whole. I enjoy roasting
whole fish in the oven or on the barbecue. Anything
cooked on the bone is juicier and more flavorful. Also,
it's a dramatic presentation.

Stuffing the cavity of the fish keeps it moist and adds
flavor. Here's a simple stuffing I like:

A few onions, sliced
1-2 fennel bulbs, sliced
Juice and grated zest of a few lemons, plus a few thin
       lemon slices
Extra-virgin olive oil
Salt and pepper
1 whole salmon or black cod (5-8 pounds), cleaned
Chopped fresh herbs
Grey or kosher salt
Cilantro and parsley sprigs, for garnish
Scallions, slivered, for garnish

Place the onions and fennel in a bowl and mix by hand.
Add the lemon juice and zest, enough olive oil to coat, and
salt and pepper to taste.

Rinse the fish, inside and out. Coat the cavity with some
olive oil and generously season with salt and pepper. Stuff
the cavity with the onion and fennel mixture.

Make a few shallow slits in the skin along both sides of the
fish (see photo) about 4 inches apart, beginning at the head
and moving toward the tail.

Rub some of your favorite herbs, a
little salt, and olive oil into the slits.
Place some lemon slices in the slits.

The slits on the fish will be wider
after cooking. You can slip a large
spoon between the flesh and the
skeleton and a piece will come right
off. When the first side has been
devoured, grab the tail and *gently*
pull the skeleton toward the head.
Watch it just pull away from the
other side of the fish. Then snip the
spine near the head, and the bottom
side of the fish is ready to go. Dig in.

Now you're ready for the grill or the oven. You can cook anything inside or outside.

For the barbecue, your fire should be low, not flaming up. A nice bed of hot coals is what you want, and a very seasoned (oiled) grate. When cooking a whole fish on your barbecue, once it's down it's down, meaning it needs to be there for about 5 to 7 minutes before you move or flip it. Letting the fish cook on one side lets it get crisp, which makes it an easier flip. Slide two long spatulas under the fish, one below the head and one above the tail, and roll the fish over. Cook for another 10 to 20 minutes. Grilling a whole fish over the fire takes a little finesse for sure. But after you do it a time or two, you will get the hang of it. The larger the fish, the more difficult it is to handle, and cooking time varies with the size and temperature of the fire.

For the oven, preheat to 375°F. Lay the prepared fish on a foil-lined sheet pan. Laying foil on the pan makes for easier cleanup; no need to oil the foil. No need to flip the fish, either. It will take about 5 minutes per pound.

To serve, place the fish on a platter. Drizzle a little olive oil over the top and sprinkle with a good-quality salt such as grey salt or kosher. Serve with Skillet-Roasted Clams (page 76) or Cider-Steamed Clams (page 78). Arrange the clams and the juice around the fish on the platter. Garnish with fresh cilantro and parsley and slivered scallions.

Salade Niçoise

This is a classic salad from the South of France. What you use in it is really up to you. It's *always* about what the garden is producing. Traditionally, this dish is served with canned tuna, but I prefer fresh albacore.

I can't give you a recipe — it depends on the market and what looks good to you. What's especially fun about this dish is that you can add your own special touches. Maybe edible flowers or squash blossoms. This can be made into a beautiful platter as well as an individual plate.

Plan on approximately 4 ounces of fish and a handful of different veggies per person. Everything is served cold except the tuna.

Green beans, blanched
Baby carrots, blanched
New red or fingerling potatoes
Extra-virgin olive oil
Whole-grain mustard
Albacore tuna
Salt and pepper
Radishes, sliced
Tomatoes, sliced
Niçoise olives (pits okay)
Hard-boiled eggs, sliced
Roasted beets (page 34)
Romesco Sauce (page 205) (optional)

Black cod, salmon, or halibut can also be used, but I prefer albacore because I can get it from a sustainable fishery.

Any vegetable that you don't want to eat raw, such as the green beans and carrots, simply blanch in boiling salted water for just a minute or two, and then refresh under cold water. You want all your vegetables fresh and crispy.

To prepare the potatoes, simply boil them in salted water until soft (approximately 10 minutes), drain, and let cool a bit. While they are still warm, slice them and rub with a little olive oil and mustard.

To prepare the albacore, season the 4-ounce piece of fish with salt and pepper. In a sauté pan just large enough to hold your fish without crowding the pan too much, heat olive oil to coat over medium to medium-high heat. Add the fish and cook for 2 minutes on each side. I like my fish rare. If you don't, then cook it longer.

Arrange your vegetables, olives, and eggs on the top half of a plate or platter. Slice the tuna with a sharp knife and fan under the vegetables at the bottom of the plate. Top with a little Romesco Sauce if you like, or drizzle with just a little olive oil.

I live in the Northwest, where the best cherries grow. The Rainier and Bing are our claim to fame. They are very different from the tart pie cherries I grew up with back East. These cherries are big, bold, and beautiful. The texture is meaty and snappy, with the perfect amount of sweetness. The best way to eat them is just as they are, but combining them with fresh summer herbs is also fantastic. Have fun and experiment with the different mints and basils that are often available. This "salad" is an excellent accompaniment to roasted chicken, lamb, and pork sausages. I also really enjoy it with a great piece of cheese and salty ham such as Serrano or prosciutto.

Cherry, Basil, and Mint Salad
Serves 3 to 4

3-4 handfuls fresh sweet cherries
1 small sweet onion, thinly sliced
A few torn basil and mint leaves
Pinch of crushed red pepper
Grated zest of 1 orange
Extra-virgin olive oil
Fleur de sel or another great-tasting salt
Black pepper

Wash the cherries, cut in half, and remove the pits. Place in a bowl and add the onion, basil and mint leaves, crushed red pepper, and orange zest.

Drizzle the salad with a generous amount of olive oil. Season with fleur de sel and a few turns of the pepper grinder. Toss gently.

Fennel, Orange, and Olive Salad
Serves 4 to 6

2 fennel bulbs, sliced as thin as you can with a sharp knife or mandoline
6 radishes, sliced thin
2 oranges, zest grated, then peeled and cut into ¼-inch slices
½ red onion, thinly sliced
Pitted olives of your choice
Extra-virgin olive oil
1-3 teaspoons fresh lemon juice or vinegar
Salt and pepper
Fresh flat-leaf parsley, for garnish

In a bowl, combine the fennel, radishes, orange slices, onion, and olives.

Add enough olive oil to coat, the orange zest, and fresh lemon juice or vinegar to taste. Stir to mix.

Season to taste with a little salt and pepper. Garnish with parsley.

Salsa Verde
Makes 2 to 3 cups

The Italians love combinations of fresh herbs. Try this nice lively condiment on just about anything. Place it in a jar and tuck in the fridge, then pull it out to add to pasta, soups, chicken, and fish.

These are approximate measurements. Feel free to change the ratios, as I do when my garden and my refrigerator need a good clearing out of a variety of herbs. In most cases, 2 ounces of herbs is equivalent to about 2 bunches.

Soft herb stems, like those on basil and flat-leaf parsley, are fine to use in a condiment like this if they are not too large; otherwise they'll be tough.

4 garlic cloves, minced
2 ounces flat-leaf parsley
2 ounces cilantro (stems are fine)
2 ounces basil leaves
1 ounce tarragon or a small bunch
1 ounce mint leaves
Juice and grated zest of 1 large lemon
Extra-virgin olive oil
Salt to taste
1 medium onion, grated
1 fennel bulb, grated
4 tablespoons capers, rinsed and chopped if large

I never waste anything. When a recipe calls for lemon or orange juice, I always zest it first and incorporate it into the dish I am making.

The easiest way to do this is in a blender or food processor. Add everything but the onion, fennel, and capers. Pulse into a nice relish consistency, adding enough olive oil for a texture like runny pesto. My personal preference is not too smooth.

Mix in the onion, fennel, and capers with a spatula. Pop it into the fridge in a sealed glass container; it will be fine for a week or two.

A vessel can inspire a dish; it really is a part of the meal, the enjoyment, the process. We start with what we are serving. How will I prepare it? How will it be presented, and where will we eat it? If we do not engage with all our choices, we do miss something. I have always loved big bowls and platters. For me, big bowls help the food rise up. It does not look flat. Your plates and bowls are like a canvas. You can bring all the nurturing and goodness of food and serve it beautifully. Maybe you serve a meal in a bowl or on a plate you found at a thrift shop, but it is a dish you just love. You do miss something eating on the go or eating out of Styrofoam or plastic — these things are not real.

I've been working with a ceramic artist, Jamil Scherief, who gave me bowls to play with, suggesting that the container or plate we eat from should be given as much attention as the food it holds.

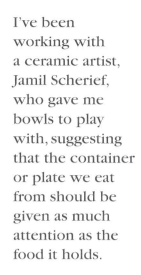

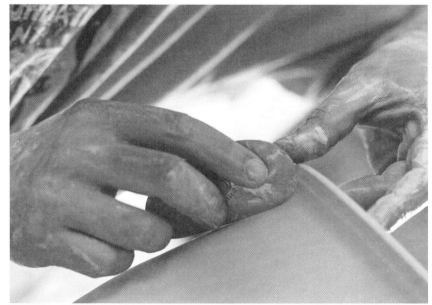

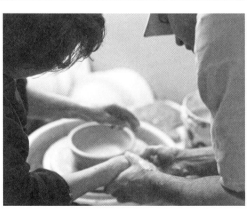

When the
berries are ripe
and ready, it is
time to gather
and eat as many
as you can.
I also love to
freeze berries.
In the middle
of winter, having
fresh frozen
blueberries on
my hot cereal
or granola
makes my day.

Strawberry Prosecco Soup
Serves 4 to 6

This little "soup" is a fun intermezzo or palate cleanser that's always a nice surprise when I entertain in the summer.

2 pints fresh organic strawberries
Juice of 1 lime
Juice of 1 orange
Salt
2 cups Prosecco (Italian sparkling white wine)
Fresh mint, chopped
Fresh basil, chopped
Black pepper

Stem and gently wash the whole berries. Place in a blender with the citrus juices and a pinch of salt. Blend until very smooth. This can be done ahead of time.

Now comes the fun part that we do at home. Divide the pureed strawberries among 4 to 6 chilled bowls — about ½ cup in each. Then go around the table and add some Prosecco to each bowl. Scatter lots of mint and basil all over the soup. Give the pepper grinder a couple of cranks over the top. *Buon appetito!*

Blueberry and Goat Cheese Galette
Serves 6

Sweet Rich Shortcrust (page 121)
Parchment paper
3-4 cups blueberries
1 tablespoon sugar
Juice and grated zest of 1 lemon
Pinch of salt
1 teaspoon cornstarch
½ cup soft goat cheese
1 large egg
Raw sugar
1 tablespoon unsalted butter
Basil Syrup, for serving

Prepare the Sweet Rich Shortcrust. Line a baking sheet with parchment paper. In a bowl, combine the blueberries, sugar, lemon juice and zest, and salt. Add the cornstarch and toss to coat the blueberries evenly.

Roll out the crust in a circular shape so that it is about ¼ inch thick. Trim the edges to even out the crust, but since this is a rustic dessert, it's fine if the edges are not perfect. Transfer the crust to the baking sheet.

Pile the blueberries in the center of the crust, leaving a 2-inch border. Crumble the goat cheese evenly over the blueberries.

Beat the egg lightly. Paint the edges of the crust with the egg. Fold the edges about an inch in toward the center of the galette. Chill for 20 minutes.

Preheat the oven to 375°F.

Brush the crust with egg and sprinkle with raw sugar. For extra richness, dot butter over the blueberries. Bake until the crust is golden, about 30 to 40 minutes. Serve warm or at room temperature with Basil Syrup.

Basil Syrup
Makes about 1 cup

½ cup sugar
1 cup cold water
1 cup fresh basil leaves (packed)

Combine the sugar and water in a saucepan and cook over medium heat, stirring, until the sugar is dissolved.

Add the basil, stirring to ensure that all the leaves are submerged. Lower the heat and simmer for about 20 minutes. Remove the basil. If necessary, cook the liquid at a low boil until it is syrupy.

I like to drizzle this over fresh berries and ice cream.

Lemon Curd with Fresh Berries
Serves 4

3 large eggs
4 large egg yolks
1 cup sugar
1 cup fresh lemon juice
¼ pound unsalted butter, melted
Pinch of salt
Fresh berries, for serving
Confectioners' sugar, for garnish

When summer is in full swing and fresh berries are plentiful, this lemon curd is quick and easy. The tart lemon really showcases the sweetness of the berries. I use this more like a sauce, with local berries as the star.

Combine the eggs, egg yolks, and sugar in a medium saucepan and whip until thick and pale yellow. Add the lemon juice, melted butter, and salt.

Cook over low heat, stirring, until it *just* coats the back of a spoon. If you want it more like a pudding, cook it a little longer. Strain to get any lumps out and let it cool to room temperature.

Drizzle over a bowlful of berries, or serve as a curd garnished with berries. Dust with confectioners' sugar.

Citrus-Olive Oil Cake with Fresh Berries
Serves 6

Nonstick cooking spray
2 large eggs
1¼ cups sugar
Grated zest of 1 orange and 1 lemon
1¼ cups flour
¾ teaspoon baking powder
¾ teaspoon baking soda
Pinch of salt
¾ cup extra-virgin olive oil
¾ cup whole milk
Crème fraîche and fresh berries, for serving

Preheat the oven to 325°F. Coat an 8-inch cake pan with cooking spray.

In a stand mixer, whisk the eggs and sugar until pale and fluffy.

In a separate bowl, combine the orange and lemon zest with the dry ingredients.

With the mixer running, add the oil to the egg mixture in a slow, steady stream. Next add the milk in the same fashion. Finally, add the dry ingredients and mix just enough to incorporate. The cake batter will be fairly thin.

Pour the batter into the pan and set immediately in the oven to bake. Set a timer for 15 minutes and then rotate the pan and bake for 10 to 15 minutes more, or until golden brown and coming away from the edges of the pan. Remove from the oven and let cool briefly. Run a knife around the edge of the pan to release the cake.

Serve with crème fraîche and berries.

Blackberry and Fennel Tart

Serves 4 to 6

I like pairing sweet and savory. Fennel has an anise flavor that I think goes well with the sweet and tart flavors of blackberries.

Rich Shortcrust
Parchment paper
3 small to medium fresh fennel bulbs
2 pints blackberries
1 tablespoon honey
Juice and grated zest of 1 small orange
Salt
1 egg, lightly beaten
Raw sugar
Crème fraîche, for serving (optional)
Blackberry Syrup, for serving (optional)

This can also be made as four 6-inch tarts.

Prepare the Rich Shortcrust.

Preheat the oven to 350°F. Line a baking sheet with parchment paper.

With a sharp knife or mandoline, thinly slice the fennel. Blanch in boiling salted water for just a minute. Refresh under cold running water and pat dry.

In a bowl combine the blanched fennel, berries, honey, and orange juice and zest. Gently mix. Season with just a pinch of salt.

Roll out the pastry dough so that it is about ¼ inch thick and as close to a circle as possible. Trim the edges to even out the circle, but since this is a rustic dessert, it's fine if the crust is not perfect. Transfer the crust to the baking sheet.

Spread the fennel/blackberry mixture over the pastry, leaving a 2-inch border. Fold the edges of the dough over the filling. Brush the crust with a little beaten egg and sprinkle a little raw sugar over all.

Bake for 30 to 40 minutes, or until the crust is golden brown. Serve warm or at room temperature with crème fraîche or Blackberry Syrup.

Blackberry Syrup

Prepare Basil Syrup (page 114), then add 1 cup of blackberries to the finished syrup. Leave it rustic, or if you prefer it strained, add the berries at the same time as the basil, following the same steps to completion.

Rich Shortcrust

2 cups all-purpose flour
1 cup unsalted butter, chilled and cut
      into a small dice
½ teaspoon salt
2 large egg yolks
4-8 tablespoons ice water

In a food processor, combine the flour, butter, and salt. Pulse until the butter is broken up into pea-sized bits. Transfer to a large mixing bowl.

Mix the yolks with 4 tablespoons of ice water and pour over the flour, stirring with the flat side of a cutlery knife to evenly distribute. Use the side of the knife to begin pressing the dough together, turning the bowl as you move. Add more water as needed to bring the dough together, 1 to 2 tablespoons at a time. When the dough looks like it will come together, use your hands to gently knead it into a disk.

Wrap the dough in plastic and let it rest in the fridge for at least 30 minutes before rolling it out.

Note: For a sweet crust, simply add 2 tablespoons of sugar to the flour mixture.

The key to a tender crust is to not overmix.

Honey-Roasted Peaches

Serves 4 to 6

4 ripe peaches
8 teaspoons butter
8 teaspoons honey
Salt
4 fresh thyme sprigs
Whipped cream and Raspberry Granita,
      or vanilla ice cream (optional)

Preheat the oven to 375°F.

Halve and pit the peaches. Place the peaches cut-side up in a roasting pan. Put 1 teaspoon of butter in the center of each peach half and then top with 1 teaspoon of honey. Sprinkle each peach with a small pinch of salt. Place the thyme sprigs in the pan.

Roast for approximately 15 to 20 minutes, or until the peaches are tender and the honey has caramelized. If you're pressed for time, you can broil them instead.

Serve the peaches warm or at room temperature with whipped cream and Raspberry Granita, or just simply with vanilla ice cream.

Raspberry Granita

Serves 4 to 6

3 cups raspberries
½ cup sugar
½ cup water
Pinch of salt
Juice and grated zest of 1 orange
Grated zest of 1 lemon
Juice of ½ lemon

Combine all of the ingredients in a saucepan and cook gently until the raspberries break down.

Puree the mixture and strain through a fine-mesh sieve. Taste for sweetness and adjust with orange or lemon juice and sugar.

Transfer the puree to a large shallow dish and place in the freezer. Every 20 to 30 minutes, drag a fork through the forming ice to create flaky crystals. Continue this process until the granita is totally frozen.

Serve the granita on its own or with Honey-Roasted Peaches.

Mascarpone Cheesecake with Fresh Apricot Compote
Serves 8

Nonstick cooking spray
1½ cups pistachios
3 tablespoons butter
2 tablespoons sugar
Pinch of salt

1½ pounds cream cheese, at room temperature
½ pound mascarpone, at room temperature
⅔ cup sugar
2 large eggs
1 large egg yolk
1 teaspoon vanilla extract
1 teaspoon fresh lemon juice
Grated zest of 1 lemon

Special equipment: 8-inch springform pan

Preheat the oven to 325°F. Coat the pan with cooking spray. To toast the pistachios, place in a single layer in a pan and bake, stirring occasionally, for 5 to 10 minutes, or until slightly golden and fragrant. Let cool, then crush.

First, prepare the crust. Melt the butter. In a bowl, combine the pistachios, sugar, and salt. Pour the melted butter over the pistachios and stir to blend. The mixture will be thick and almost like a paste. Press the crust mixture into the bottom of the prepared pan. Bake until the crust is golden brown, approximately 10 minutes. Set aside to cool.

To prepare the filling, in a stand mixer beat the cream cheese and mascarpone until the mixture is smooth. Add the sugar and continue to mix. Add the eggs one at a time, then the yolk. Finally, add the vanilla, lemon juice, and zest. Be sure to scrape the bottom of the bowl with a spatula to ensure that the mixture is well blended. Pour the cheesecake batter into the pan on top of the cooled crust.

Bake the cheesecake for 20 to 30 minutes, or until it is set on the top and has a uniform wobble when gently shaken. Bake for a few more minutes if necessary. Remove from the oven and let cool on a rack to room temperature; then refrigerate for 30 minutes to set. Serve with Fresh Apricot Compote.

Fresh Apricot Compote

8 ripe apricots
1 tablespoon unsalted butter
¼ cup sugar
½ cup dry white wine
½ cup orange juice
Pinch of salt
1 cinnamon stick
1 bay leaf
1 tablespoon fresh lemon juice
      (optional)

Halve and pit the apricots. Cut the halves into eighths.

In a medium saucepan or sauté pan, melt the butter over medium-high heat. When it is foaming, add the apricots and toss to coat. Sprinkle the sugar evenly over the fruit and cook, stirring to prevent sticking. As the sugar begins to caramelize, pour the wine into the pan. Add the orange juice, salt, cinnamon stick, and bay leaf. Simmer gently for 10 minutes, or until the fruit begins to soften and break down.

Taste for sweetness and adjust as needed. Add the lemon juice if the compote is too sweet. Remove from the heat. Discard the cinnamon stick and bay leaf. Serve warm or cold.

For a variation, 1 to 2 cups of blueberries, strawberries, or blackberries would also work well.

Minted Cucumber Soup
Serves 4

2 cucumbers, peeled, seeded, and chopped
2 garlic cloves, minced
¼ cup mint leaves
½ cup cilantro leaves
2 tablespoons rice wine vinegar
Pinch of crushed red pepper
1 teaspoon ground cumin, plus more for garnish
Juice and grated zest of 1 lemon
1½ cups plain yogurt
Salt and pepper

In a food processor, combine the cucumbers, garlic, mint, cilantro, vinegar, red pepper, cumin, and lemon juice and zest. Process until smooth. Add the yogurt and blend. Season to taste with salt and pepper.

Refrigerate the soup until chilled.

To serve, pour the soup into bowls. Sprinkle a little cumin on top.

Sometimes we forget how good simple things can be.

Grilled Apricots with Blue Cheese and Serrano Ham

You can serve these tasty bites right off the grill as an hors d'oeuvre just as they are, or toss up a nice fresh salad using your favorite salad greens and serve the apricots alongside or on top. Also feel free to use any blue cheese you like. Prosciutto works just fine if you can't find Serrano ham.

1-2 apricots per person
1 teaspoon of your favorite blue cheese for each apricot
2 paper-thin slices of Serrano ham or prosciutto per apricot
Skewers for grilling (see note)
Extra-virgin olive oil or Balsamic Syrup (page 132)
Salt and pepper
Fresh thyme leaves

Halve the apricots and remove the pits. Place the apricots on a sheet pan and put ½ teaspoon of blue cheese in the center of each apricot half. Wrap a slice of ham around each apricot half so it covers the cheese.

Preheat the grill. Be sure to oil the rack first to prevent sticking.

Slip a few of the apricots onto a skewer for easy turning. Place the apricots, filled side down, on the hot seasoned grill for about a minute, simply warming the cheese and lightly crisping the ham. Turn them over and let sit for about another minute.

To cook these in the oven, preheat to 350°F. Place the apricots on a sheet pan, filling side up, and bake for about 7 minutes.

To serve, place the apricots on a platter and drizzle with a bit of olive oil or Balsamic Syrup. Season to taste with salt and pepper, and sprinkle with thyme leaves.

Note: If using wooden skewers, be sure to soak them in water for at least an hour to prevent burning on the grill.

Grilled Radicchio with Goat Cheese and Balsamic Syrup

Serves 4 to 8

4 heads of radicchio
Good-quality extra-virgin olive oil
Salt and pepper
6-8 ounces fresh goat cheese, cut into bite-size pieces
Loads of fresh seasonal herbs, leaves removed from the stems (thyme, basil, oregano)

Heat the grill to medium.

To prepare the radicchio for grilling, remove any wilted outer leaves, then slice each head in half from stem to end. Lightly oil the grill as well as the radicchio.

Place the halves cut-side down on the grill for a few seconds, or until you see a light char on the leaves. Using a pair of tongs, turn the heads over and grill for another few seconds. Keep a close eye, as it will go quickly — no more than 2 minutes total — and you don't want the radicchio to burn. Remove from the grill and lay the halves on a platter.

Season to taste with salt and pepper and drizzle with a little more olive oil. Garnish with the cheese and herbs. To serve, drizzle with Balsamic Syrup.

When fresh figs are in season, try adding them to this salad.

Balsamic Syrup

1 cup balsamic vinegar
1 cup fresh orange juice (optional)

For the basic version, pour the vinegar into a saucepan. Cook over low heat until reduced by half. Remove from the heat and let cool.

For a kicked-up version, add a cup of fresh orange juice to the cup of vinegar and cook until reduced by half.

This is really good on ice cream and strawberries, peaches, or other stone fruits. It's also a nice garnish for cheeses. Especially a blue. The sweetness adds a nice accent to the salty blue.

Roasted Grapes, Olives, and Walnuts

I love this little snack, and it is so easy. The sweet juices of the grapes, the earthy richness of the walnuts, and the saltiness of the olives are a great combination. This mix is delicious with all kinds of cheese, but I particularly like a Spanish blue cheese called Cabrales.

½ cup picholine olives
½ cup oil-cured olives
½ cup Kalamata olives
1 cup seedless red grapes
¼ cup walnut halves or Spanish almonds
¼ cup fresh thyme leaves (see note)
Good-quality olive oil

Preheat the oven to 350°F.

In a bowl, combine the olives, grapes, nuts, and thyme. Drizzle with a generous amount of olive oil and stir to coat.

Spread the mixture on a sheet pan. Roast in the oven for about 15 minutes, or until heated through and the grapes are juicy but not mushy. Serve immediately. This is also good as leftovers the next day — just reheat in the oven or on the stove or barbecue.

Note: Take a handful of fresh thyme sprigs and slide your fingers down the stem in the direction opposite to the way the herb grows. You will get a nice little pile of thyme leaves.

Grapes are also fun to grill. Preheat a slotted pan on the barbecue. Add the grape mixture and grill for about a minute, tossing once or twice. Or you can oil the whole cluster of grapes and grill them directly on your barbecue to add to the plate. Either way, you just want to bring out the juiciness — but keep them firm — and smoke them a bit. If you're not grilling over a wood fire, be sure to add some wood chips to your barbecue for that delicious smoky flavor.

It's probably obvious to you that I like to grill. There is something so delicious about those subtle smoky flavors. I like a nice peach just picked off the tree as much as anyone else, but here is something you should try. The arugula has a soft peppery taste that mingles very nicely with the sweet peach. The dressing gives it the zing that brings it all together.

I would really recommend that you head off to a farmers' market and get your peaches and herbs there. They will taste so much better. If your peaches are from a local farmer, then this salad will still be delicious without grilling the peaches. Just season with salt and pepper to your liking.

Grilled Peaches with Arugula and Serrano Ham
Serves 4

2-3 really nice tasty peaches, not overly ripe
Extra-virgin olive oil
About 3 cups arugula (a little stem on the arugula is fine)
2 small bunches *each* basil and mint
Spiced Orange Vinaigrette
Salt and pepper
Serrano ham – a few thin slices per person
Goat cheese – just enough to keep it interesting

Preheat the grill.

Slice the peaches in half and remove the pits. Drizzle the peaches with some olive oil and lightly grill them, cut-side down.

In a salad bowl, mix together the arugula and the basil and mint leaves. Quarter the grilled peaches and add to the salad mixture. Drizzle with a generous amount of Spiced Orange Vinaigrette and salt and pepper to taste. Toss.

Gently gather as much salad as you can in your hands and let it fall and spread onto a platter. Garnish with the ham and goat cheese. To serve individually, do the same thing on each plate.

This is more than just a variation of a basic vinaigrette. It's all about orange.

Spiced Orange Vinaigrette
Makes about 1 cup

1 cup fresh orange juice, plus the grated zest
Juice and grated zest of 1 lime
1 teaspoon crushed red pepper
1 shallot, finely diced
2-3 sprigs of fresh mint, leaves removed and torn
Several sprigs of fresh thyme, leaves removed
¼ cup extra-virgin olive oil
Salt

Place the juices in a small saucepan and bring to a light boil over medium-high heat. Add the crushed red pepper and shallot and cook until reduced by half. Remove from the heat.

Add the mint and thyme leaves and the zest. Slowly whisk in the olive oil. Add salt to taste.

Don't forget to use the zest — it adds a whole different flavor.

Grilled or Roasted Broccoli with Prosciutto and Roasted Pepper
Serves 4 to 6

I eat broccoli only when it's from the farmers' market. I need to add interesting flavors to really enjoy it. I like it best grilled.

1 medium head of broccoli
Salt
Extra-virgin olive oil
A few thin slices of prosciutto or Parma ham, cut into bite-size pieces
1 roasted red bell pepper, sliced
Parmigiano-Reggiano cheese, shaved into curls
Pine nuts, almonds, or hazelnuts (optional)
Fresh lemon juice
Orange segments, for garnish

Preheat the grill.

Cut the head of broccoli lengthwise into 4 to 6 pieces, leaving most of the stem.

Bring a pot of salted water to a boil. Add the broccoli and cook for 1 minute. Refresh in an ice bath or under very cold running water. Drain and pat dry. Drizzle with olive oil and grill for 3 to 5 minutes, turning often.

Transfer the broccoli to a bowl and add the prosciutto, roasted pepper, and Parmigiano-Reggiano curls. Nuts add a nice flavor. Squeeze on lemon juice and drizzle with olive oil. Mix gently.

Arrange the salad on plates and garnish with orange segments.

You can also roast the broccoli on a sheet pan in a 400°F oven for about 7 minutes — no need to blanch.

The broccoli I buy from the farmers does not have the tough woody stems that you typically find in a supermarket. Everything but the very end is usually quite tender.

Grilled Romaine with Anchovies and Parmigiano-Reggiano

I truly enjoy making dishes at home that I can serve family style. This is a grilled summer salad that looks awesome on a platter. There is something about generous platters of food that always makes an impression. Family style gives a more casual feeling to the dinner table and brings us together nicely. Another bonus is that there is less stress in making one plate look good rather than six.

How much you make is totally up to you. I can eat a whole head of this. A nice glass of white wine with this salad on the patio in the summer is perfect. Romaine is a great lettuce that stands up to the grill. This is my version of an easy summer Caesar salad.

Romaine lettuce
Salt and pepper
Anchovies
Fresh lemon juice
Good-quality olive oil
Parmigiano-Reggiano cheese

Preheat the grill.

Remove the outer leaves of the romaine. If the head is big, slice it lengthwise into 4 or 5 spears.

Lightly oil the grill. Place the romaine spears on the grill for a few seconds, or until you see a light char here and there. Season to taste with salt and pepper.

Lay the spears casually out on a platter and add your favorite anchovies — use as many as you like. Generously drizzle the lemon juice and olive oil over the leaves. Grate Parmigiano-Reggiano all over the top. A few turns of the pepper grinder, and you're good to go. Don't forget the bread and wine!

Vegetables Grilled over the Fire (Escalivada)

You certainly can make this at any time of the year, but it's best in the summer because there are so many beautiful fresh vegetables at the farmers' market. Use your imagination and remember that almost anything can be grilled, including green beans, broccoli, carrots, and mushrooms.

The fun part of this dish is to slice some of your vegetables differently from one another and have different textures. For instance, slice the green zucchini lengthwise and the yellow squash on the bias. Add a handful of green beans to the mix. Have fun and however you slice it, it will be perfect.

These different-colored vegetables make an impressive platter. I am also a believer that when the grill is fired up, I may as well cook everything on it and make it worthwhile. Simple dishes can be made with the leftovers during the next few days, and most of your work is done.

Here are some suggestions for the dish and what I used for the photograph:

Zucchini
Yellow squash
Fennel
Sweet onion
Different kinds of peppers
Eggplant
Scallions, trimmed
Extra-virgin olive oil
Salt and pepper

Preheat the grill to get it nice and hot.

Slice up the zucchini, yellow squash, fennel, onion, and peppers about ½ inch thick. Cut the eggplant a little thinner so it gets crispy. Leave the scallions whole.

Place the veggies in a mixing bowl and drizzle with a little olive oil. Season with salt and pepper. Get your hands in there and mix it all up.

Take a few handfuls of veggies at a time and fill the grill, making sure everything has a place to sit directly on the grate. Don't disturb them for a few minutes even if there is a bit of a flare-up. Then use a large metal spatula or a pair of long tongs to flip the veggies. Let them sit there for another few minutes. When things are looking cooked, scoop them into a pan. Repeat the process. If there are some vegetables that you think could be a bit crispier, put them back on the grill. Serve with Skordalia (page 145).

Here are some ways I like to use these grilled vegetables for a quick start to a meal during the rest of the week. We don't have to start everything from scratch each time we cook. I certainly don't. And this is exactly what I do at home:

Pasta with Grilled Vegetables and Fresh Herbs

This is a great summer dish that I like to eat at room temperature.

Your favorite pasta
Extra-virgin olive oil
Grilled vegetables (page 141)
Fresh mint, basil, parsley, or any other fresh herbs
Fresh tomatoes (optional)
Freshly grated Parmigiano-Reggiano cheese or fresh goat cheese (optional)
Chimichurri (page 147) (optional)

Cook the pasta in boiling salted water. Drain and refresh under cold water. Transfer to a bowl and drizzle lots of olive oil all over the pasta.

Rough-chop your grilled vegetables and toss them with the pasta. Tear up lots of fresh herbs and add to the mixture. Toss it all together.

You can add tomatoes or anything else fresh you like. A little grated Parmigiano-Reggiano or fresh goat cheese is a nice addition. Mix in some chimichurri if you want a little zip!

Grilled Vegetable Panini

Focaccia
Grilled vegetables (page 141)
Chimichurri (page 147)
Fresh basil leaves
Goat cheese

Heat a sauté pan or a griddle, or your barbecue if you like. Make this just as you would a grilled cheese sandwich, but with your grilled vegetables.

Skordalia

This makes about 4 cups, which will serve 6 to 8. The recipe can be easily cut in half.

Basically, skordalia is a garlicky Greek potato dip. Think mashed potatoes with no cream but with lots of garlic, swimming in delicious olive oil. It's simple and can be a really nice side with fish or meat, as well as a great underlay for Vegetables Grilled over the Fire (Escalivada) (page 141).

1 pound potatoes (Yukons are good, but russets will work just as well)
1 cup really good extra-virgin olive oil
A handful or two of peeled garlic cloves, depending on how garlicky you like it
Dash of fresh lemon juice and grated zest
Salt and pepper

Peel the potatoes and cook in boiling salted water until tender. Drain. It's best to boil the potatoes whole to prevent them from getting waterlogged and gooey.

Heat some of the olive oil in a sauté pan over low heat. Add the garlic and cook until it softens, watching carefully to ensure that it doesn't brown. Remove the garlic from the pan; reserve the oil.

Put the potatoes and garlic through a food mill or ricer, or smash with a potato masher.

Add the remaining olive oil, the oil from sautéing the garlic, the lemon juice and zest, and salt and pepper to taste. Stir to blend. Serve warm or at room temperature.

This condiment is an Argentinean staple. There are many versions of chimichurri. I like it piquant, with a nice round citrus flavor and loads of fresh herbs. I make chimichurri when I grill vegetables, and then I have it for them and anything else I want to use it on. It will jazz up just about anything you are cooking: rice, pasta, meat, fish, and sandwiches. It's a good thing to have in your fridge.

Chimichurri
Makes about 2 cups

About 1 cup extra-virgin olive oil, plus
    more for grilling peppers
4 hot peppers, such as red Fresno,
    jalapeño, or serrano
2 garlic cloves
Juice and grated zest of 1 lemon
1 teaspoon ground cumin
½ teaspoon hot smoked paprika
A generous handful of parsley, chopped
A generous handful of cilantro, chopped
Salt

Lightly oil and grill the peppers until they
are slightly charred (page 221). For this
recipe, I don't bother seeding or skinning
them. Just remove the tough stem.

In a food processor or blender, pulse the
grilled peppers and garlic until roughly
chopped. Add the lemon juice and zest,
cumin, and paprika. Pulse until blended.

Add about a cup of olive oil. Toss in the
chopped herbs and mix it all up. Don't
overmix; it should be chunky. Adjust the
seasoning to taste, adding salt or more
lemon juice if you think it needs it.

A food processor can make it a bit easier than a blender to keep the texture chunky. Using a
mortar and pestle to make chimichurri is another option. It takes a little more time, but it's very
authentic, and I love to get in there and grind everything up. The oils are released, intensifying all
the flavors.

Roasted Garlic

I use garlic in so many things. Truthfully, I think it should be roasted most of the time. It's so good in vinaigrettes, soups, salads, pastas, and marinades. Even at home, I typically roast a pound or two at a time, and then I have it on hand for a couple of weeks.

Because we use so much at the restaurants, we peel enough garlic for a week and then roast it, all covered with olive oil, in a 300°F oven until it's soft and slightly caramelized.

I roast garlic at home slightly differently. Pick whichever way works better for you. On Sunday morning, set your oven to 250°F. Place a number of whole, unpeeled garlic heads in a baking dish. It's good to have them fit snugly. Add enough olive oil to come about a quarter of the way up the sides of the garlic. If you have some herbs on hand such as rosemary or thyme, go ahead and add a few sprigs. Cover tightly with aluminum foil. Bake for a few hours, or until the garlic is nice and soft.

Once the garlic is roasted, just pinch it out of its skin into a container with a little of the oil to keep it moist, and put it in the refrigerator to use throughout the week. It's not going to go bad. You can rub it on your chicken, rub it on your fish, or — one of my favorites — spread some on a crostini and top with chopped fresh tomatoes. Simple, but delicious.

Also remember to save all of the oil from roasting. Then use it for sautéing, add it to salad dressings and marinades, or drizzle a little on soup or pasta. It's *all* good. At the restaurants we use the leftover "roasted garlic oil" in a potato-garlic sauce called Skordalia (page 145).

An easy way to peel lots of fresh garlic:

This is something that kids can do — they love it. Smash the head of garlic on the kitchen counter (root end up) to break apart the cloves, then put them in a bucket of water overnight. The next day, squeeze the ends of the little cloves and watch them pop out of their skins just as roasted garlic does. Once you have peeled the garlic, place it in a jar, pour in enough olive oil to cover it, and refrigerate. Fresh peeled garlic stored this way will keep for a couple of weeks.

Fresh Beans

When fresh green,
yellow wax, and purple
beans are available at
the farmers' market,
by all means buy them.
Supermarket beans are
typically tough and not
very good. Good-quality
beans have a bright color
and snap easily when
broken. Look for beans
with immature seeds.
Young beans with enough
fuzz to cling to one's
shirt are usually tender.
Large swollen seeds in
string beans foretell
a tough bean.

CERTIFIED ORGANIC

`haricot verts`
Green Beans
$5 $\frac{50}{=}$ per pound

Sauté or blanch the beans, and then use them in all sorts of different ways later on in the week. Add blanched beans to cold salads, for example. I like to combine thinly sliced raw peppers (a mix of hot, mild, and sweet) and a rainbow of bean colors. It's like a party on a plate! Here is a recipe that I really enjoy.

Fresh Market Beans with Anchovies, Sweet Peppers, and Basil
Serves 6

1 pound beans, stem ends snipped
3-5 tablespoons extra-virgin olive oil
3 garlic cloves, peeled and crushed
1-2 anchovy fillets, smashed to release the oils
1 red, yellow, or other sweet pepper, seeded and sliced into strips about ¼ to ½ inch wide
Pinch of crushed red pepper
Juice and grated zest of 1 lemon
Salt and pepper
1 bunch of basil, leaves removed and torn
Grated orange zest (optional)

Bring a large pot of salted water to a boil. Drop the beans in and cook for 3 minutes. Drain and refresh under icy water. Drain the beans and dry off with a paper towel.

In a large sauté pan, heat the olive oil over low heat (remember to heat your pan first). Add the garlic and anchovies. Cook slowly until the garlic is golden, about 10 minutes. The longer you can leave the garlic and anchovies in the oil, the more they perfume the oil. Remove the garlic and anchovies from the pan with a slotted spoon. Set aside and let cool. Then chop or mince into a paste to add to the beans later.

Add the sliced peppers and crushed red pepper to the pan and cook over low heat for 5 minutes, or until the peppers soften (a little crunch is good). Add the beans and heat until just warmed through (they are already cooked). Again, texture here is important; I like them slightly crunchy. Stir in the garlic/anchovy mixture and lemon juice. Add salt and pepper to taste. Toss in the basil leaves and give it a good stir.

Transfer to a serving platter and top with the fresh lemon zest. This is nice with orange zest as well.

If you have a lot of beans, try pickling them. I like to pickle them whole and raw. The acid in the pickling juice "cooks" the beans. I snip them on one end (leaving the tail on), add them to the jar "tail up," and then add the hot pickling liquid according to the Pickled Celery recipe (page 248).

Braised Belgian Endive

I think Belgian endive is an underutilized and underappreciated vegetable. Like leeks, it grows under the ground, which is why its tulip-shaped leaves remain mostly white. Although I enjoy it raw in salads, I like it braised as well. This is delicious with roasted meats.

Belgian endives
Unsalted butter
Salt and pepper

Slice the endives in half lengthwise. In a sauté pan large enough to hold the endives in one layer, melt enough butter over low heat to generously cover the bottom of the pan. Lay the "inside flesh" of the endives flat onto the butter. As the butter slowly browns, spoon it over the top of the endives. This way you are braising the top. The bottom will caramelize and become sweet. Do this for about 10 minutes, or until tender. Season to taste with a little salt and pepper.

My Pizza Dough
Serves 4 as an appetizer, or 2 to 4 as an entrée

There are many recipes for pizza dough. If you have a favorite, use it. Otherwise, here is mine. It also can be used as a type of pita bread.

¾ cup lukewarm water
1 envelope active dry yeast
2 cups high-gluten flour (all-purpose is also okay)
1 teaspoon sugar
1 teaspoon salt
1 tablespoon extra-virgin olive oil, plus more for coating
      the bowl

Combine the lukewarm water and yeast in a bowl. Let sit for 5 minutes. This step is called proofing, to test that the yeast is still good. The water turns cloudy as the active yeast grows and bubbles, which means your dough will rise.

In a food processor (if you have one), blend the flour, sugar, and salt.

Add the yeast mixture and olive oil to the processor and blend until a sticky ball forms. Transfer to a floured surface and knead the dough by hand until it is nice and smooth.

Oil a mixing bowl and add the dough ball, turning to coat with the oil. Cover with plastic wrap and let sit until it doubles in size (about an hour). Punch the dough down. At this point, you can either use it or wrap it in plastic and store in the refrigerator or freezer.

Grilled Pizza

Heat your grill to about 325°F or medium heat.

On a floured surface, stretch and shape your fresh pizza dough into a round or oblong shape. It can be as thick or thin as you like, ranging from about 8 to 11 or 12 inches in diameter. Lay the dough on the grill. Do not disturb it for a few minutes — wait till bubbles begin to form on top of the dough. With a spatula (or with your fingers if they are not too sensitive), flip the dough over. Lower the heat. While the second side is down, brush the top of the pizza dough with olive oil and scatter your prepared toppings over the oiled crust. Sprinkle with a bit of grated Parmesan or mozzarella. Close the grill lid and cook for about 5 minutes, or until the toppings are hot and the cheese has melted.

Grilling pizza is fun outdoor cooking and it's easy. You can also do this in a pan in the oven.

To cook your pizza indoors, preheat the oven to 400°F. On the stovetop over low heat, warm a lightly oiled ovenproof sauté pan that's roughly the same size as your stretched pizza dough. Add the stretched dough to the pan. Quickly add your chosen toppings. Place the pizza (still in the pan) on the bottom rack of the oven for about 15 minutes, or until the crust is browned. If you would like your pizza toppings to be a little browned, grill under a low broiler for 5 to 10 minutes, or until golden.

Some of my favorite farmers' market toppings are Vegetables Grilled over the Fire (page 141) and these two:

Caramelized Onion and Roasted Beet Pizzetta

4 medium-sized yellow onions
Extra-virgin olive oil
4-5 garlic cloves, peeled and slivered
4-6 medium-sized beets (it doesn't matter what color), roasted, peeled, and sliced about ⅛ inch thick
      (see Oven-Roasted Beets, page 34)
Goat cheese
Fresh thyme leaves

Peel the onions and slice in half. Then *thinly* slice the halves.

Heat a large sauté pan over low heat. Add enough olive oil to coat the bottom of the pan. Add the onions and the slivered garlic to the pan and cook on *low* heat, stirring occasionally, for about an hour, or until very soft and golden brown. This will make 3 cups or so.

When you've flipped and oiled your pizza dough, spread the caramelized onions over the crust. Then add the sliced roasted beets, overlapping in a circle. Add a little goat cheese to the top and some freshly picked thyme. Finish per usual on the grill or in the oven for about 12 minutes, browning the cheese.

Grilled Wild Mushroom Pizzetta

½ pound wild mushrooms, cleaned and sliced
Extra-virgin olive oil
Salt and pepper
1 tablespoon *each* (more or less) chopped fresh rosemary
        and fresh thyme leaves
½ cup grated mozzarella
2 tablespoons grated Parmigiano-Reggiano cheese

Preheat the oven to 450°F.

Lay the sliced mushrooms on a sheet pan. Drizzle with a generous amount of olive oil and season well with salt and pepper. Sprinkle with the rosemary and thyme. Roast in the oven for about 10 to 15 minutes, or until browned and crispy.

When you've flipped and oiled your pizza dough, scatter the roasted mushrooms over the top. Sprinkle with the grated mozzarella and Parmigiano-Reggiano. Close the grill lid. Cook for about 5 minutes, or until the mushrooms are hot and the cheese has melted.

Grilled Porcini with Arugula and Parmigiano-Reggiano
Serves 6 to 8 as a side dish, or 4 as an entrée

1 pound fresh porcini mushrooms
Extra-virgin olive oil
Salt and pepper
1 bunch of arugula
Fresh lemon juice
Parmigiano-Reggiano or any hard farmers' market cheese

Porcini are the king of mushrooms. For me, grilled is best. Here is what I like.

Heat up your grill.

Slice the porcini as thick as you like. The thicker they are, the better — they will have a meatier texture. Spoon a little olive oil over each slice and season to taste with salt and pepper. Grill for a few minutes on each side, or until tender.

Meanwhile, place the arugula in a salad bowl. Add lemon juice, salt and pepper, and olive oil to taste. Toss to mix.

Lay the grilled porcini flat on a plate and arrange the arugula leaves on top or beside them. Use a vegetable peeler to shave generous strips of cheese over the top.

Chanterelle Soup

Serves 4 to 6

2 tablespoons extra-virgin olive oil
1 tablespoon unsalted butter, plus a little more for finishing the soup
2 garlic cloves, minced
1 small onion or 1 medium shallot, diced
1 leek, diced
2 sprigs of thyme, leaves removed
½ pound chanterelles, cleaned (see note)
1 tablespoon red wine vinegar
½ cup dry white wine
3-4 cups vegetable or chicken stock, enough to cover
1 cup cubed bread – baguette or similar rustic white
1 cup heavy cream
Salt and pepper

Heat the olive oil and 1 tablespoon butter in a soup pot over low heat. Add the garlic, onion, leek, and thyme leaves and sweat until soft.

Add the chanterelles and cook for a minute or two. Then add the vinegar and cook for another 20 minutes or so, until the chanterelles are soft.

Add the wine and cook until reduced by half. Add enough stock to cover the mushrooms and simmer for 15 minutes.

Add the bread cubes and cook until very soft, about 10 minutes. Stir in the cream.

Transfer the mixture to a blender and puree. Return to the pot and heat gently. Finish with a little butter. Season to taste with salt and pepper. Serve hot.

Note: To clean the chanterelles, use a small brush or wipe with a paper towel.

Serve this rich and filling soup with bread and a salad for a complete meal.

Wild Mushrooms Roasted in Parchment
Serves 3 to 4

This is a fantastic way to roast mushrooms. I even do this when I'm camping.

½ pound of your favorite fresh wild mushrooms, cleaned and
     sliced or quartered
Sprig of fresh thyme
2 garlic cloves, crushed
2 tablespoons extra-virgin olive oil
Salt and pepper to taste
18-by-18-inch square of parchment paper

Preheat the oven to 450°F.

Place all the ingredients in the center of the parchment paper. Fold the edges, making sure they are sealed.

Place the packet on a baking sheet and bake for about 20 minutes. Slide the packet onto a plate and pierce just before serving.

Wild mushrooms can be a bit dirty and also delicate. I've found that good foragers will often clean them up before they land on their market tables. Sometimes a little more cleaning is necessary. Keep them as dry as possible, as mushrooms can absorb water. Wipe them clean with a brush. For more stubborn dirt, rub it off with a paper towel. Mushrooms roast best when they are clean and dry.

Morels

These are my favorite mushrooms. They are very versatile and have a nice woodsy flavor. The larger ones are great for stuffing. If you're just going to sauté morels, cut them into rings (which is an attractive method), quarter them, or simply leave them whole. I am not a fan of slicing them too thin because after they are cooked, you can't tell what they are, even though the flavor is still very intense.

Whichever you do, first clean the morels by placing them in a large bowl of cold water. Bounce them up and down in the water to dislodge the dirt that may be in the crevices. Then scoop the mushrooms out of the water with your hands, leaving the dirt in the *bottom* of the bowl. If you turn the whole thing out into a strainer, then you just pour the dirt back over them — a common error.

Spread a layer of paper towels on a sheet pan and place the morels on them to dry. They can just sit on your counter for a couple of hours or overnight.

To get the cleaned morels ready for stuffing, take a small paring knife and gently cut away *some* of the stem but not all. It depends on how big the mushroom stem is. You need just enough room for your fingers to push in the savory mixture. A little gentleness and patience is required so you don't tear the mushroom. If you do tear one, just chop it up and put it in your cheese mixture.

Stuffed Morels with Browned Sage Butter and Cherries

Serves 1

The woodsy flavor of morels is a wonderful combination with cherries. Morels and cherries can be found in the Northwest at around the same time of year. I accidentally came up with this unusual but delicious combination when I had extra morels and cherries in my cooler. I stuffed the morels with a bit of goat cheese, baked them for about 10 minutes, and served them with the cherries and fresh arugula. It was an instant hit.

A couple of large fresh morel mushrooms, cleaned
1 ounce or so of soft cheese such as goat cheese or ricotta
Extra-virgin olive oil
Salt and pepper
Browned Sage Butter (page 62)
A few cherries, halved and pitted
A pinch or two of arugula
Crusty bread, for serving

Preheat the oven to 350°F.

Fill the morels with the cheese (your hands work best). Place on a baking sheet and drizzle with olive oil to coat. Season to taste with salt and pepper. Bake for 10 minutes, or just until soft.

Prepare the Browned Sage Butter. Add the pitted cherries and stir. Season to taste with salt and pepper.

To serve, place the baked morels on a layer of arugula. Spoon the Browned Sage Butter over the morels. Serve on or with crusty bread.

Chefs are often asked what their last meal would be. I don't know why, but at least 50 percent of the time, the answer is roast chicken and some sort of potato, usually mashed. I find it interesting that no matter what type of food a chef is known for, the inherent knowledge is that food's main purpose is to nourish us, not impress us.

This humble bird does just that. I am a true believer that chickens from a conscientious and caring farmer who raises them in a humane environment taste better, and also that purchasing them instead of commercially grown birds is the right thing to do.

Tamara's Roasted Chicken
Serves 4 to 6

3 fresh lemons
8 garlic cloves, peeled and smashed
4-5 sprigs rosemary, needles removed and chopped (thyme, savory, and bay leaf are great too!)
Salt
½ cup extra-virgin olive oil, plus more for drizzling
1 whole bird
Pepper
Melted butter (optional)
Rosemary sprigs, lemon ends and wedges, and garlic cloves, for stuffing (optional)

Thinly slice the lemons. Remove the seeds, then roughly chop the lemons. With a mortar and pestle, working in batches, grind the garlic, rosemary, lemon, and a generous pinch of salt. Add the olive oil a little at a time, until the mixture is chunky like a relish. You can also do this with your chef's knife or by pulsing in a food processor if you don't have a mortar and pestle. If you're planning to make Lemon Chicken Risotto (page 172) with the leftover chicken, set aside 3 tablespoons of the relish.

Begin stuffing the chicken by gently lifting the skin from the breast and adding the relish. You can even work your way down to the legs and the thighs. We call this "loving the chicken." Sounds kind of fun, huh? Finish by rubbing the chicken inside and out with the remainder of the paste. Season the outside of the bird with about 2 palms-full (approximately 1½ tablespoons) of salt and some pepper — as much as you like.

Drizzle a little olive oil or melted butter inside your chicken. I always stuff rosemary sprigs, lemon ends and wedges, and more garlic cloves in the cavity if I have extra, before popping it in the oven. After the chicken is roasted, save these, along with the carcass, to make stock for Lemon Chicken Risotto (page 172).

Preheat the oven to 400°F.

Place the chicken breast-side up in a roasting pan and roast for 10 minutes. The chicken will be just starting to brown, firm up, and seal in the juices. Then turn the oven down to 325°F and roast for about another 45 minutes. Baste throughout roasting.

The chicken will take on average about 18 minutes a pound. The leg should feel loose when you jiggle it. Also, you can pierce the flesh between the thigh and the breast to see if the juices run clear. Let the chicken rest for 15 to 20 minutes before slicing to keep the juices in.

Lemon Chicken Risotto
Serves 4 to 6

I received my first bit of training in a French kitchen, where *nothing* goes to waste. After I get all the meat removed for my chicken dinner, I immediately put the carcass, the rib-cage bones, etc., in a pot and cover with cold water. I add the garlic, rosemary, and lemon pieces from inside the roasted chicken and bring it all to a boil. I let it simmer while we're eating our roast chicken dinner, then strain it after dinner and pop the stock in the fridge.

The next day there will be some fat that firms up at the top of your container. Okay, you can throw it away, but I use it to sauté the onions for my Lemon Chicken Risotto. Here's what I do:

3 tablespoons chicken fat or olive oil
1 cup diced onions
1 cup Arborio rice
½ cup dry white wine
4-5 cups homemade chicken stock, heated
Leftover roast chicken, cut into bite-size pieces (approximately 2 cups)
3 tablespoons leftover lemon relish from Tamara's Roasted Chicken (page 170)
Pinch of salt
2 tablespoons unsalted butter (optional)
2 tablespoons heavy cream (optional)
½ cup freshly grated Parmigiano-Reggiano cheese
Grated orange zest and fresh parsley, for garnish

Heat the chicken fat or olive oil in a large sauté pan over medium heat. Add the onions and cook until translucent. Add the rice and cook for a few minutes, stirring so all the rice gets coated.

Then add the wine. When that is absorbed, add 1 cup of the hot chicken stock and cook, stirring, until the liquid is absorbed. Continue adding the stock 1 cup at a time after the previous one has been absorbed. (So you'll need to make about 4 to 5 cups of stock the night before just to be safe.) Cook until the rice is just a little al dente. Then stir in your leftover chicken, lemon relish, and salt.

If you want it really creamy, add the butter and cream and give it a good stir. Don't forget to grate some Parmigiano-Reggiano on top before serving. Garnish with orange zest and parsley.

Try shallots in place of onions for a slightly different flavor. Shallots are so sweet when they're freshly dug.

Risotto Base
Serves 4 to 6

A special rice called Arborio is often used in making risotto. This rice is glutinous, and there's no need to rinse it. The idea behind risotto is that the slow addition of liquid and constant stirring create a creamy texture. Always use a wooden spoon, never a metal one. Stirring bursts the shells of the kernels of rice, which allows the starch to be released. See how it gets creamy when you stir it. If you didn't stir it, this wouldn't happen.

4 cups chicken, vegetable, or beef stock
1 tablespoon unsalted butter
1 tablespoon extra-virgin olive oil
¼ cup chopped onion
1 cup Arborio rice

Here's a way to make cooking risotto quick and easy. This is how we do it in my restaurants.

In a saucepan, heat the stock to a simmer.

In a large sauté pan, heat the butter and olive oil over medium heat. I like to use a sauté pan rather than an upright pot because the larger surface area is easier to work with and minimizes the stirring time. Add the onion to the pan and sauté until translucent. Add the rice and stir to coat well.

Over low to medium-low heat, add the simmering stock to the rice 1 cup at a time, stirring the rice constantly until the liquid is absorbed before adding more. It will be done in about 20 minutes. The rice should be slightly underdone, not mushy. Try not to overcook it.

If you'd like to prepare this ahead of time, stop cooking after 3 cups of stock have been absorbed. Remove the risotto from the stove, spread it on a sheet pan, cover, and place in the refrigerator. It will keep for 3 to 4 days.

When you're ready to use it, heat the remaining stock in a saucepan. Warm the risotto in a large sauté pan over low heat. Stir in the hot stock and other ingredients and cook until creamy.

Risotto with Farmers' Market Shell Beans, Spinach, and Bacon
Serves 4 to 6

The stars here are the fresh shell beans from the farmers' market. Once you taste these, you will have a tough time going back to the commercial dried beans that we have become used to eating.

8 bacon slices, or more if you like
1 cup or more of simmering chicken or vegetable stock or water
Risotto Base, partially prepared with 3 cups of stock (page 173)
1-2 cups fresh shell beans, cooked until al dente (see notes)
3 large bunches of spinach, stems removed
½ cup grated pecorino cheese, plus more for topping
1 bunch of thyme, leaves removed
Juice and grated zest of ½ lemon
Salt and pepper

I have to admit that when I make this one, I render the diced bacon in the same pan I am ultimately going to use to make the finished risotto. In my kitchen, no pork-products flavor will be wasted. Bacon is part of my holy trinity, along with salt and olive oil.

So go ahead and chop the bacon, and put it in a 10-inch-or-so sauté pan. Cook it slowly to get it nice and crispy. Pour off the excess fat as it accumulates, and save it for a rainy day or when you make Spinach Salad with Wild Mushrooms and Goat Cheese (page 42).

Once the bacon is crispy, scoop it out of the pan and set aside. Humor me and leave a little of that tasty bacon fat in the pan. Over medium-low heat, add ½ cup of the heated stock, and the prepared rice. Stir. Add about another ½ cup of the stock, stirring constantly until all the liquid is absorbed. Add the beans and heat through.

When things are looking creamy and delicious, your risotto is ready to serve. Add the fresh spinach leaves, pecorino, thyme leaves, and lemon juice and zest; give it a good stir and season to taste with salt and pepper.

Serve the risotto in warm bowls. Top with crumbled bacon and more grated pecorino. *Buon appetito!*

Two pounds of fresh dried shell beans in the pod will yield approximately ½ to 1 cup of shelled beans, depending on the size of the pod.

To cook dried beans, use a ratio of 3 cups beans to 4 cups water. Bring to a boil, then turn down to a simmer. Add 2 bay leaves and/or a clove of garlic. Simmer for about 20 minutes, or until al dente. This can be done ahead of time, if you'd like.

Farmers' market shell beans take about half as much time to cook as commercial dried beans. You don't have to soak them because they are not as old and dry.

Roasted Butternut Squash, Chanterelle, and Sage Risotto
Serves 4 to 6

1 medium butternut squash
4 tablespoons unsalted butter, divided
Salt and pepper
Extra-virgin olive oil
2 cups chanterelles or other wild mushrooms (about ¼ pound)
⅓ cup chopped onion
Risotto Base, partially prepared with 3 cups of stock (page 173)
½ cup dry white wine
1 cup or more of simmering vegetable or chicken stock
3-4 tablespoons chopped fresh sage
½ cup grated Parmigiano-Reggiano cheese
4-5 bacon slices, fried until crisp and crumbled

First prepare the squash. Preheat the oven to 350°F. Slice the squash lengthwise down the middle and remove the seeds. Dab 2 tablespoons of butter on the squash. Season generously with salt and pepper. Place cut-side up in a pan and roast for about 1 hour, or until soft. Remove the pulp and puree it. Season to taste with salt and pepper. Set aside.

Heat a small amount of olive oil or butter in a sauté pan over medium-low heat. Add the chanterelles and cook, stirring, for about 5 minutes, or until tender. Season to taste with salt and pepper. Set aside.

In a large sauté pan, heat 2 tablespoons olive oil over medium to medium-low heat. Add the onion and cook until translucent. Add the prepared rice. Stir. Add the wine, stirring constantly until the wine is absorbed. Add the heated stock, about ½ cup at a time, stirring constantly until all the liquid is absorbed.

Stir in the squash puree and the chanterelles. Then add the sage and grated Parmigiano-Reggiano. Taste for seasoning. Just before serving, stir in 2 tablespoons of cold butter. Spoon into warm bowls and garnish with bacon.

Squash Blossoms

Squash blossoms are always a showstopper at the markets. But buyer beware: they last only a few hours. On the day you buy them, you should use them. When you get the blossoms home, gently wrap them in moist paper towels and place in the fridge. Frying the blossoms is a popular method. They also can be used to make a simple, light summer soup.

Fried Stuffed Squash Blossoms
Serves 4

I love to dip these in a light batter that gets them really crunchy. Here's a basic tempura batter for about 12 to 15 blossoms:

TEMPURA BATTER
1 cup all-purpose flour, or substitute corn flour for more crunch
½ teaspoon baking powder
½ teaspoon salt
1 large egg
1½ cups ice-cold water or club soda (it will make the batter more airy)

FILLING
1 cup ricotta, or 1 cup ricotta and grated mild cheese such as Monterey Jack or soft goat, or 1 cup of a blend of all three
1 poblano, pasilla, or other green chile, roasted, seeded, and chopped
1 tablespoon chopped fresh parsley
1 teaspoon chopped fresh cilantro
Salt

12-15 squash blossoms
Extra-virgin olive oil, for frying

To prepare the batter, sift the flour, baking powder, and salt together in a bowl.

In another bowl, beat the egg, then blend in the ice-cold water. Gently mix in the dry ingredients; lumps are okay. Refrigerate the batter until you are ready to use it.

To prepare the filling, combine the cheese, chile, parsley, cilantro, and salt to taste in a bowl. Mix until blended.

Stuff each squash blossom with about 1 tablespoon of filling, gently pushing it toward the stem. Twist the top of the flower so the filling doesn't fall out.

Pour enough olive oil into a large sauté pan to cover the bottom. Heat over medium-high heat. Before frying, test the oil by carefully putting a drop of batter in it. If it sizzles, it's ready.

Roll each stuffed squash blossom in the batter to coat. Working in batches, fry the blossoms for a couple of minutes on one side, then gently turn and continue frying on the second side, or until golden brown. Remove to paper towels and season to taste with salt.

You can also deep-fry these, submerging the blossoms entirely in the oil. This requires more oil, which can be a bit costly and is not for everyone. You want a pan that can hold enough oil to submerge the blossoms yet not overflow. Heat the oil to 350°F and fry the blossoms until golden brown.

Serve immediately as is, or with Five-Minute Fresh Garden Tomato and Herb Sauce (page 59) or Spiced Orange Vinaigrette (page 137), or use as a garnish for Squash Blossom Soup.

Squash Blossom Soup
Serves 4

3 tablespoons butter, plus 2 tablespoons cold butter
3 shallots, minced
3 garlic cloves, minced
1 leek, trimmed, washed, and diced
15-20 squash blossoms, julienned
2 cups vegetable or chicken stock
½ cup dry white wine
½ cup heavy cream
Salt and pepper

Melt 3 tablespoons of butter in a saucepan over medium heat. Add the shallots, garlic, and leeks and sauté until soft and translucent.

Add the squash blossoms, stock, and wine. Simmer over medium-low heat for about 10 minutes.

Transfer the mixture to a blender and puree. Blend in the 2 tablespoons of cold butter. Transfer back to your pan, add the cream, and cook over low heat until warm. Season to taste with salt and pepper.

To serve, place a fried squash blossom in each serving bowl and pour some soup around it.

Pumpkin Soup
Makes 2 quarts

Fall and winter are favorite times of year for cooks because we braise everything from meats to vegetables. The smells fill our kitchens, and we spend more time thinking about and preparing our meals. Imagine on a Sunday filling up the house with the aroma of soup simmering on the stove or roasting meats and vegetables in the oven — very comforting.

The markets are loaded with different pumpkins and squashes in the fall. You can use either squash or pumpkin (which is also a squash) in this recipe. There are so many to choose from. Butternut is a really nice one. You will notice that squashes have different levels of starch, so you will have to adjust the liquid accordingly. The only way to become familiar with the varieties is to split them open, remove the pulp and seeds, and roast them.

Preheat the oven to 350°F. With your hands or a knife, break up the cleaned squash into easy-to-handle chunks. Place on a baking pan, season generously with salt and pepper, and dab with butter. Roast for about an hour, or until the flesh is tender. When the squash is cool, scrape the flesh off the skin. (This is something you can do ahead and refrigerate.)

For each pound or so of roasted flesh:
Extra-virgin olive oil
1 onion, sliced
2 medium carrots, diced
3 garlic cloves, minced
1 red bell pepper, seeded and chopped
6-8 cups vegetable or chicken stock
2-4 tablespoons heavy cream (optional)
Salt and pepper
Crème fraîche (or sour cream if you can't find it), for garnish
Seasoned roasted pumpkin seeds (page 193), for garnish

Heat a glug or two of olive oil in a large soup pot over low heat. Add the onions, carrots, garlic, and bell pepper. Cook for about 15 minutes, or until soft and translucent.

Add the roasted pumpkin or squash and the stock. Stir. Bring to a simmer, then cover and continue to simmer for 30 minutes, or until all the vegetables are very soft. Remove from the heat and let cool.

Working in batches, fill the blender halfway with the mixture and blend until very smooth. With the blender running, add some of the heavy cream and blend for 1 minute longer. This will give the soup a nice soft and silky texture.

A good rule of thumb is to have about 2 inches or more of liquid over the vegetables in the blender to achieve a good consistency. Use this method for all pureed soups. Some squashes have more starch, so you may need a little more liquid than with other vegetables. Adjust accordingly. A pureed soup should be a little thicker than a cream sauce. Be sure to season to taste with salt and pepper.

Reheat the soup and pour into bowls. Top each serving with a dollop of crème fraîche and some seasoned roasted pumpkin seeds. This soup can also be served cold.

Pumpkin Steamed Puddings
Serves 6

6 ounces unsalted butter, plus more for greasing ramekins, at room temperature
6 tablespoons Lyle's Golden Syrup, plus extra for serving (you can also use
    Grade B maple syrup)
¾ cup sugar
3 large eggs
¾ cup flour
1 teaspoon baking powder
1 cup pureed roasted pumpkin (page 184)
Whipped cream, for serving

Special equipment: Six 4- to 6-ounce ramekins

Butter the ramekins and place 1 tablespoon of golden syrup in each one.

Preheat the oven to 325°F.

In a stand mixer, cream the butter and sugar. Add the eggs one at a time, incorporating each fully before adding the next.

In a separate bowl, combine the flour and baking powder. Mixing slowly, add the dry ingredients to the butter mixture. Gently fold in the pumpkin puree.

Spoon the mixture evenly into the ramekins, about ¾ full. Place the ramekins in a roasting pan and add enough hot water to reach halfway up the sides of the ramekins. Cover with foil and place in the oven for 45 to 60 minutes. Rotate the pan after 30 minutes. The puddings are done when they have puffed up slightly and the tops are firm to the touch. Remove from the oven and let cool for 5 minutes.

Turn the puddings out onto plates and serve with whipped cream and warm golden syrup over the top.

This recipe can also be made in a bundt pan instead of individual ramekins. Butter the pan and fill the bottom with the golden syrup. Spoon the pumpkin mixture into the pan and cover tightly with foil. Place the pan in a pot large enough to hold it with a lid over the top, and fill the pot halfway with water. Keeping the water at a low simmer, cover the pot and steam the pudding in the oven for an hour.

Fall and Winter Squash

There are often many varieties of fall and winter squashes gracing our farmers' tables, and it can be a challenge to decide which one to choose. My advice is to just ask — your farmer will most likely be happy to describe the different textures and flavors. Some of the more popular varieties are acorn, butternut, delicata, and spaghetti. One thing to know is that you can roast all of them in a similar way and enjoy them equally. The biggest differences will be the texture and the level of sweetness. Cooking times will vary just a little. They are all done when a fork or skewer pierces the squash easily.

Spaghetti squash looks like a yellow football. Not many people know what to do with it, but it's a great vegetable. Cook it whole, without splitting it. Just place it on a sheet pan and pop into a 350°F oven. When it is soft to the prick of a fork, it's ready to go. Split the squash in half, scoop out the seeds, and use a fork to gently scrape out the flesh. It will come in long strands — you guessed it — just like spaghetti. Add a little butter and salt and pepper.

Butternut is
the sweetest.
Start by roasting
it, then you can
make a soup,
puree, or filling.
The puree goes
nicely with
duck breast . . .

Brown Sugar and Balsamic Squash

Whether it's butternut, spaghetti, kabocha, pumpkin, or acorn — no matter.

Squash
Butter
Brown sugar
Balsamic vinegar
Salt and pepper

Preheat the oven to 350°F.

Split the squash in half. Scrape out the seeds and reserve them.

Select a roasting pan that the squash will fit into comfortably. Melt enough butter to give you ¼ inch in the pan. Add some brown sugar and drizzle vinegar over the sugared butter mixture. Sprinkle the squash with salt and pepper. Lay the squash in the pan, cut side down. Bake for about an hour, depending on the variety, or until the squash is soft and golden brown.

Scoop away the flesh from the skin with a large spoon and place in a mixing bowl; add the drippings from the pan if you'd like. Use a hand potato masher to press down on the squash a few times for a rustic puree. Season to taste with salt and pepper.

Roasted Squash Seeds

While your squash is roasting, place the seeds in a bowl of cold water and use your hands to rub off the pulp. Place the seeds on a baking sheet and bake in the oven along with the squash for about 5 to 10 minutes. No seasoning yet — that just dries them out. Remove from the oven and toss the hot roasted seeds with a bit of salt and smoked paprika. Use as a garnish for Pumpkin Soup (page 184) or a snack.

Eating seasonally really keeps cooking simple.

Cappelletti with Browned Sage Butter with Hazelnuts

Serves 4 to 6 as a starter, or 3 to 4 as an entrée

Cappelletti (meaning "little hat" in Italian) is something I typically make on a day when I have more time. I usually prepare a large batch, freeze them individually on a flour-dusted sheet pan, and then place them in a sealed container in the freezer to use as I like. They will easily store for a few weeks. Below are two of my favorite fillings.

Roasted Butternut Squash Filling

1 medium-sized butternut squash
2 tablespoons brown sugar
Salt and pepper
2 tablespoons unsalted butter, cut
    into small pieces
2 tablespoons mascarpone cheese
2 tablespoons ricotta cheese

Preheat the oven to 350°F.

Split the squash in half lengthwise and remove the seeds. Sprinkle the brown sugar and salt and pepper all over the squash flesh. Evenly dot with the butter. Roast the squash cut-side up in a shallow baking pan for about an hour, or until it is soft.

Scoop out the squash and place in a food processor. Add the mascarpone and ricotta and blend until totally creamy. Season to taste. Chill the filling thoroughly in the refrigerator before making your stuffed pasta.

Swiss Chard and Ricotta Filling

1 pound or a big bunch of Swiss chard, stems removed
1 cup drained ricotta
1 large egg
Salt and pepper

Blanch the chard in boiling salted water for 1 minute, or until the leaves are bright green. Remove with tongs and place in ice water. When chilled, drain and chop fine. Place the chopped chard in a towel and squeeze dry.

Transfer the chard to a bowl and add the drained ricotta, egg, and salt and pepper to taste. Stir until well blended. Chill the filling thoroughly in the refrigerator before making your stuffed pasta.

TO MAKE THE CAPPELLETTI
Parchment paper
Flour, for dusting
1 pound of your favorite fresh pasta dough
        (makes 15 to 25 cappelletti)
3-inch round cookie cutter
1 egg, beaten with a drop or two of water
Freshly grated Parmigiano-Reggiano cheese, for serving

Line a half sheet pan with parchment paper and dust generously with flour. Set aside.

Roll out the pasta into very thin sheets (or purchase sheets of pasta). Cut into circles with the cookie cutter.

Place roughly 1 teaspoon of chilled filling just a little off-center on each circle (a bit closer to the bottom of the circle). Lightly brush some beaten egg on the rim of the circle. Fold over in a half-moon shape and seal the edges. Bring the corners together and pinch.

Lay the cappelletti on the prepared pan in a single layer so that none of them are touching. Place in the freezer for about an hour, or until frozen (they cook better when frozen). You can cook them at this point or transfer to a ziplock bag for later use.

Bring a large pot of salted water to a boil. Working in batches, add the frozen cappelletti to the water and cook at a gentle boil for a few minutes. When they float to the surface, they are ready. Check to make sure the filling is not still frozen.

Drain the cappelletti and place immediately in the warm Browned Sage Butter, tossing gently to coat. Spoon into bowls and grate fresh Parmigiano-Reggiano on top. Serve immediately.

Browned Sage Butter with Hazelnuts

3 tablespoons unsalted butter
1 tablespoon chopped fresh sage
1 teaspoon fresh lemon juice
2 tablespoons crushed toasted
        hazelnuts
Dash of salt

Heat a large sauté pan over low heat. Add the butter and cook until very brown and bubbly, about 3 minutes. Add the sage. Remove from the heat. Stir in the lemon juice and hazelnuts. Season with salt.

Deep-green leaves of Swiss chard are so beautiful at the farmers' market. Not only are they good for you, but they are also delicious. The rainbow variety, with its red, golden, and white stems, is my favorite. Be sure to use the stems unless they are so large that they're tough. Just nip off the very bottom of the stalk.

Swiss Chard with Garlicky Chickpeas (Garbanzo Beans)
Serves 4 to 6

GARBANZO BEANS
1 cup or more garbanzo beans, drained (canned are fine)
5 garlic cloves, peeled
1 sweet onion or 2 large shallots, sliced thin
2 bay leaves
Extra-virgin olive oil to coat

SWISS CHARD
2 bunches of Swiss chard
2 tablespoons extra-virgin olive oil
2 garlic cloves, peeled and crushed
Juice and grated zest of 1 small lemon
Salt and pepper

Toasted almonds, for garnish (optional)
Feta or aged goat cheese, for garnish (optional)

This Mediterranean version is a very tasty antipasto or side dish.

Preheat the oven to 350°F.

To prepare the garbanzo beans, combine all the ingredients in a shallow baking dish. Cover with foil. Bake until the garlic is fork-tender, approximately 30 minutes. This can be done ahead of time. Just leave everything in the baking dish until you are ready to use it; or you can refrigerate it to use another day.

To prepare the chard, nip off the bottom of the stalks or woody ends. Slice the stems into small bite-size pieces with a sharp knife up to the leaf. Tear the leaves into larger bite-size pieces. Wash in cold water. Drain and dry off with paper towels to avoid splattering when the greens hit the oil.

Heat a sauté pan over low heat, then add the olive oil. Add the crushed garlic and brown to perfume the oil. Remove and discard the garlic. Add the Swiss chard and cook for a few minutes, just until wilted. Add the lemon juice and zest, and season to taste with salt and pepper. Remove from the pan.

While you're wilting the chard, if the beans are chilled, warm them in a 350°F oven for about 10 minutes.

Combine the wilted chard mixture with the garbanzo bean mixture. Season to taste with more salt and pepper. Remove the bay leaves and transfer to a white platter. To add a bit more texture and taste, garnish with toasted almonds and a sprinkling of feta or aged goat cheese. Serve warm or at room temperature.

Root Vegetables

Root vegetables are overlooked and underrated. Any vegetable whose fruit stays in the ground the entire time is referred to as a root vegetable — carrots, potatoes, onions, rutabagas, turnips, celery root, and parsnips, to name a few. I think the root vegetables that you find in the farmers' markets are so much better than what is available elsewhere. It's no wonder people pass them up at the supermarket. That's why I thought we should spend a little time on them.

When some roots are in season, all are in season. As I said before, what grows together goes together. When I see them on the stands, I buy a variety and often roast them together on a baking sheet with herbs such as sage, rosemary, and thyme, lots of garlic, and good-quality olive oil.

Storing Root Vegetables over the Winter

Root vegetables can be easily stored in your garage, in a metal garbage can. Put some sawdust on the bottom (peat moss works too). This helps prevent the vegetables from drying out. Be sure your sawdust is from untreated wood. Arrange some potatoes or other root vegetables in a single layer. Be sure there are no rotten ones, as this will cause them all to go. Add more sawdust to cover and repeat. They will keep this way for quite some time, four to six months. This is how food was stored before refrigeration.

You can also do this in a crawl space, if you have one, or dig a pit in the earth and proceed as above. This is a good way to store foods over the winter and retain that fresh flavor, especially when you know you may not be able to make it to the farmers' market every week.

201

Roasted Root Vegetables

Preheat the oven to 400°F. Peel the vegetables you choose and cut into 1½- to 2-inch chunks. Toss with olive oil to coat and place in a single layer on a cookie sheet or roasting pan. Roast undisturbed for 20 minutes to get nice and crispy, then turn them with a spatula and let them brown on the other side for another 10 minutes. Season with a little salt before serving.

Root Vegetable Mash
Serves 4 to 6

I also enjoy these vegetables mashed up. I like to cook all of the vegetables at the same time because I've found that if I cut one in half and put the other half back in the fridge, I often will not use it, and then lose it. So if you are making this dish, think about how much you will use, unless you want to eat a lot of leftovers. You could also use the other halves in the Roasted Vegetables (page 203) I talked about.

1 small rutabaga
1 small celery root
1 parsnip or carrot, or both
2 potatoes, any kind is fine
Salt
2 tablespoons chopped fresh thyme
1 teaspoon chopped fresh sage
2 tablespoons unsalted butter, or more to taste
Pepper

Preheat the oven to 300°F.

Peel and quarter the roots. Place in 2 quarts of boiling salted water. Cook, uncovered, until soft. Drain. Lay on a sheet pan and dry in the oven for 10 minutes.

Transfer the vegetables to a bowl. Add the herbs and butter. Mash with a handheld potato masher — it doesn't have to be smooth. Season to taste with salt and pepper, adding more butter if you'd like. Keep warm until ready to use.

Romesco Sauce

Makes about 2 cups

1 teaspoon plus 1 cup extra-virgin olive oil, divided
½ cup slivered almonds
3 red bell peppers, stemmed and cut into chunks
4 large tomatoes, herb-roasted (page 53), cooled
1 large head of garlic, roasted and peeled (page 148) or sautéed (see note)
Pinch of crushed red pepper
1 tablespoon sherry vinegar or white vinegar
1 cup croutons (see note)
½ teaspoon salt
Pepper

Heat 1 teaspoon olive oil in a sauté pan over low heat. Add the almonds and toast until golden brown, about 5 minutes. Remove from the heat and let cool.

Place the almonds in a food processor and pulse until coarsely ground. Add the bell peppers, tomatoes, garlic, and crushed red pepper. Pulse. Add the vinegar and slowly add ½ cup of olive oil. Add the croutons and pulse. Add the remaining ½ cup of olive oil. Season to taste with salt and pepper.

If the sauce is too thin, add some more bread; if it's too thick, add a little vinegar and water. It should be thick and creamy, with a nutty texture. I like mine kind of chunky.

Note: Roasted garlic is one of those ingredients that elevates just about everything. You can use fresh if you don't have any roasted. The flavor will be good, but different. Just peel and crush 10 to 12 cloves of garlic and cook over low heat in 2 tablespoons olive oil until light golden brown.

Note: To make the croutons, take a couple of slices of good crusty white bread such as a baguette, cut into small cubes, and toss with a little extra-virgin olive oil and salt and pepper. Spread on a rimmed baking sheet and bake in a 325°F oven for 5 to 10 minutes, or until golden brown. This will make approximately 1 cup of croutons. The bread acts as a thickener, so a rustic loaf works perfectly. The key to good croutons is a crispy exterior and a chewy, soft interior. Don't let them get too hard.

This is a sweet pepper sauce that's delicious with fish. The Spaniards use it on their legendary fish soup. It's great with a tray of fresh farmers' market veggies. I also serve it as a condiment for roasted root vegetables in the fall.

Celery Root

Food is at its best when it's in season. The time for celery root is spring and winter, and when you can get it grown locally, it's even better. Celery root is kind of nutty and at the same time somewhat floral, with a taste reminiscent of celery. That makes it a very versatile vegetable — great to use as an accompaniment to meat or fish. Roast it or puree it. It is fantastic!

Roasted Celery Root

Celery root
Extra-virgin olive oil
Salt and pepper

Preheat the oven to 350°F.

Peel the celery root and cut into 1- to 2-inch chunks. Place in a roasting pan and toss with olive oil to coat. Season with salt and pepper.

Roast for about 30 minutes. At this point, it's soft and the full nuttiness comes through. Use it just like that, or puree it to serve alongside braised or roasted meat.

Here's a trick. Use the meat juices from your roast as part of your liquid to puree. The puree can be rustic (not smooth), or keep the blender engine running until it is silky soft. I like it especially under short ribs.

Celery Root Soup

Serves 6

4 tablespoons unsalted butter, divided
2 teaspoons extra-virgin olive oil
1 cup diced onions
2 garlic cloves, minced
2 leeks, washed and diced
2 large celery roots, peeled and chopped
4 cups chicken or vegetable stock
1 cup milk
Salt and pepper

Heat 3 tablespoons butter and the olive oil in a large saucepan or a soup pot over low heat. Add the onions, garlic, and leeks and sweat until they glisten.

Add the celery roots and stock. Cover and cook until soft. Add the milk and cook for another 10 minutes, or until heated through.

Transfer to a blender and puree. Return to the pan and reheat. Add 1 tablespoon cold butter and stir until it melts. Season to taste with salt and pepper.

Celery Root Puree — Another Way

Celery root
Milk
Butter
Salt and pepper

Peel and chop the celery root into 1-inch or so chunks. Place in a saucepan and simmer in a bit of milk and water until it is very soft. Puree it all, then add some butter and salt and pepper to taste. This is delicious served under a roasted piece of salmon.

Leeks

Leeks out of the garden are nothing like the ones you find at the supermarket. Leeks grow deep in the ground, and the part that pops up out of the soil is green. The root below is creamy white. That's the part you want.

An easy way to clean leeks:

Cut off the really green part. Compost it. If the root hasn't been trimmed, go ahead and cut that off, leaving the base intact so the leek stays together.

With a sharp knife, begin just above the root and make a series of slices lengthwise (from white to light green) that go all the way to the end of the leek. Do this in three or four places around the stalk.

Holding it by the root end, bounce the leek up and down in a bowl of cold water, letting it fan out to release the dirt. The dirt hidden in the stalk will fall to the bottom of the bowl.

To slice the leek, first cut it in half lengthwise, then cut it on the bias into slices an inch or two in length.

Creamed Leeks with Prosciutto and Parmigiano-Reggiano
Serves 6 to 8

This is almost like a carbonara sauce, only without the egg. It is really good served over pasta, in risotto, or over a chicken breast, in a variation on chicken Parmesan. It can also be mixed into scrambled eggs or served over toast points. An all-around really good sauce, it is also tasty by itself.

Parchment paper
3 tablespoons unsalted butter
2 leeks (approximately 1 pound), cleaned and sliced
2 garlic cloves, slivered
A sprig or two of fresh thyme and rosemary, chopped
Salt and freshly ground pepper
1 cup dry white wine
2 cups chicken stock
Enough prosciutto slices to cover the leeks
1 cup heavy cream
1 cup grated Parmigiano-Reggiano cheese

Preheat the oven to 325°F. Cut a piece of parchment paper to fit a 9-by-12-inch ovenproof pan.

Melt the butter in the ovenproof pan over medium heat. Remove from the heat. Brush the parchment paper with some of the melted butter; set aside.

Add the leeks, garlic, and thyme and rosemary to the pan. Season with a smidgeon of salt and pepper. Add the wine and chicken stock. There should be enough liquid to just cover the leeks. Lay the slices of prosciutto on top, overlapping to cover the leeks and just barely go up the sides of the pan. This will seal in the leeks and prevent the liquid from evaporating. It will also give the leeks a delicious flavor. Lay the parchment paper, buttered side down, on top.

Bake for about 45 minutes, or until the leeks are tender. Remove the prosciutto from the pan and dice. Transfer the leeks with a slotted spoon to a bowl and mix with the prosciutto.

Cook the liquid remaining in the pan over medium heat on the stovetop until reduced by half. Add the cream and cook for 3 minutes. Then add the leeks and Parmigiano-Reggiano cheese and simmer until thickened. You can add more butter if you like — it just depends on how the ol' ticker's going. Keep warm until ready to serve.

It's great fun to learn about a new vegetable and how to prepare it. Perhaps you have passed up the Jerusalem artichokes in mid to late summer or the kohlrabi in the fall. Learning to cook with all of the farmers' foods encourages them to grow more interesting items. It teaches us how to be better cooks and gives us a reason to play in the kitchen. It gets really boring cooking the same foods over and over again. If there is something at the market you're not familiar with, ask the farmers about it — they love to talk about their products!

Jerusalem Artichokes

Otherwise known as sunchokes, these roots are sweet raw and add a really nice crunch to any salad. They're tasty at any size. There's no need to peel them; just slice thin with a sharp knife or mandoline as you would a radish.

Or slice them a little bit thicker and sauté in butter and garlic. Season to taste with salt and pepper.

They can also be roasted whole in a 350°F oven, just like a potato. Smash them with a fork, dab with some butter, and sprinkle with fresh thyme leaves.

Parsnip Soup
Serves 6 to 8

3 tablespoons unsalted butter, divided
1 onion, diced
1 leek, washed and diced
3 garlic cloves, minced
2 pounds parsnips, peeled and sliced into ¼- to ½-inch rounds
1 quart of vegetable broth, approximately
½ cup heavy cream
Salt and pepper

Melt 2 tablespoons of butter in a soup pot over low heat. Add the onion, leek, and garlic and cook until soft and caramelized. Add the parsnips.

Add a cup of broth and continue to cook for about 15 minutes. Then add enough of the remaining broth to cover the vegetables by about 2 inches and simmer, covered, for 20 minutes, or until the parsnips are very soft. Remove from the heat and let cool.

Transfer the mixture to a blender and puree. Pour back into the pot and add the cream. Bring the soup to a simmer, then whisk in the remaining tablespoon of butter. Season to taste with salt and pepper.

Every soup such as this can also be eaten chunky and not pureed. If you plan to serve it that way, you might want to be a little more aware of how you cut your veggies so that they are attractive. This soup is really nice with a bit of hot Browned Sage Butter (page 62) drizzled over the top before serving.

Sometimes I add fried parsnips as a garnish. Then you've got something crisp.

Note: The rule of thumb for most pureed soups is that there should be at least 2 inches of liquid above the vegetables after they cook down.

Fried Parsnips Garnish

Peel parsnips into long shavings with a potato peeler. Heat ½ inch of olive oil in a sauté pan over medium-high heat. Working in batches, add some parsnip shavings to the pan and quickly fry until crispy, then remove to a paper towel. Parsnips, like other root vegetables, have a lot of sugar in them, so if you fry them too hot, they'll burn. If you live in a place like the Northwest where there's a lot of humidity, be sure to seal the fried parsnips in a ziplock bag once they're cool so they don't get soggy.

About Smoked Paprika

There's nothing like this spice, made from the same sweet red peppers found stuffed in olives. At peak ripeness, the peppers are hung to dry over an open fire, imparting the spice's distinctive smoky aroma and flavor.

My favorites are produced by the Spaniards from the La Vera region, where the climate is ideal and the process of smoke-drying follows a centuries-old tradition. Smoked paprika comes in three distinct styles: dulce (sweet), agridulce (bittersweet), or picante (hot), each with that same great smokiness.

Something essential to know about paprika is that fresh, fresh, fresh is key. If you have a tendency to use very little, just pop the sealed can in the freezer. Or buy just a little if you can get it in bulk.

About Stock

Stock is flavored water made by simmering bones and/or vegetables that is used to make sauces and soups. It is the backbone of good cooking.

You can always use roasted or caramelized vegetables in your stocks — play!

When you've had chicken for dinner, remember that the bones can be used to make a great chicken stock. Add carrots, celery, onion, parsley, leeks, fennel — whatever you have — and cover with water (a little white wine never hurts). I add aromatics such as thyme, black and white peppercorns, bay leaf, and a few cloves all tied up in cheesecloth. I may even throw in a whole chicken. This creates a great stock. Let it simmer, uncovered, on your stove for one hour or a little more. Strain it. Chill it. Ladle it into quart containers or smaller and freeze. It will be better, and you have the satisfaction of making it your own.

For vegetable stock, just leave out the bird.

No matter what you're cooking, throughout the process, taste, taste, taste.

To enjoy
and support
the farmers'
markets fully,
let's consider
learning how
to eat and cook
seasonally. This
is when food is
at its best.

Peppers are nature's way of saying I am beautiful, sweet, and delicious. To me, peppers are definitely the glamour girls of the garden. I love them roasted. Peppers roasted over a fire become sweet and smoky. When they are in abundance at the market, I crank up the barbecue and roast a whole bunch. I like to mix hot and sweet. After the peppers have cooled, I peel them (but not always), slice them (but not always), and freeze them in ziplock bags. They are great with antipasti, on sandwiches, or for a garnish with a roast or grilled meats and even fish.

Roasting Peppers

To roast peppers, I sometimes place a rack over the gas flame and set my peppers on that. Let them char on all sides and then enclose them in a paper bag or pop them in a bowl and cover with plastic wrap until they cool. Then gently remove the skins and the seeds.

Farmers' Market Sweet Pepper Soup
Serves 4 to 6

A few glugs (3-4 tablespoons) extra-virgin olive oil, plus more for drizzling
1 medium onion, diced
2-3 garlic cloves, minced
1½-2 pounds sweet peppers, roasted (page 221), peeled and chopped
½ cup fresh orange juice
1 large ripe tomato, seeded and diced
4 cups vegetable broth
3 sprigs of fresh tarragon, leaves removed and chopped
Salt and freshly ground pepper
Butter (optional)

You can use a variety of peppers, sweet or hot, whatever you like.

In a large sauté pan, heat the olive oil over medium-high heat to the point of fragrance (meaning it's not smoking, but you'll hear *tttssscchhh* when the onion hits the pan). Add the onion and garlic. Turn the heat down to medium-low and cook for about 10 minutes, or until the onion is translucent.

Add the roasted peppers, orange juice, and tomato. Cook, uncovered, for about 15 minutes, so the flavors can mingle. Add the broth and simmer for an additional 15 to 20 minutes. Remove from the heat and let cool.

Working in batches, transfer some of the mixture to a blender, filling about halfway, making sure there are equal amounts of peppers and liquid. Place the lid on the blender and pulse. (Turn the blender on and off quickly; otherwise, you may have more peppers on your counter than in the blender.) Once the veggies are more smooth than chunky, then you can blend away. When the mixture is nice and smooth, blend in the tarragon. At this point, add salt and pepper to taste.

Serve hot or at room temperature. Add a drizzle of olive oil or a dollop of butter to each bowl before serving.

You can make this without roasting the peppers. Simply sauté sliced peppers with the onions and garlic — it just gives you a different soup. You can't ruin a recipe; it's only a blueprint.

Smoky White Bean and Ham Hock Stew
Serves 4

For me, nothing is more satisfying than this stew. In the late summer, many of my farmers have fresh dried beans. Now, if that seems difficult to understand, once you have tried a *fresh* dried bean, it's really hard to go back to the *not so fresh* dried beans that we seem to be forced to use most of the year. I don't know how long those familiar white or black beans have been in those plastic packages on the grocery shelf, but I imagine it's been years! I now have a standing order with some of my farmers and pay them up front for the fresh beans they anticipate growing the following year. Storing the current year's beans throughout the winter is so satisfying and rewarding.

2 cups dried white beans
5 cups chicken or beef stock
2 sliced ham hocks
1 tablespoon tomato paste
1 medium onion, cut into chunks
4 garlic cloves, smashed
Olive oil
Chopped garlic, to taste
1 pound kale, chard, or turnip greens, chopped
Fresh lemon juice, to taste
Farm-fresh eggs, poached, for garnish (optional)
Crusty bread, for serving

Sometimes I add carrots, sometimes I don't.

In a large pot, combine the beans, stock, ham hocks, tomato paste, onion, and smashed garlic cloves. Bring to a boil, then lower the heat, cover, and simmer for about 20 minutes, or until the beans are fork-tender but still a bit al dente. Remove the ham hocks and set aside. Strain the beans, garlic, and onion from the broth. Put the broth back on the stove and cook until reduced to about 4 cups.

Heat a sauté pan over low heat, then add olive oil to coat. Add the chopped garlic and cook briefly, until fragrant. Add the greens and cook, stirring, just until wilted. Stir in the lemon juice.

Pick the ham off the bones, then slice or shred it bite-size for your stew. Add to the stock pot along with the sautéed greens, onion, garlic, and beans.

While the stew is gently heating, poach an egg to place on top of each serving. Don't forget a slice of toasted crusty bread for sopping.

The cauliflower at the farmers' markets is one of my favorite late spring/early summer vegetables. Often these heads have a purple hue that catches my eye. They are irregular in size, which is a sign that they are not commercially grown, and not as "tight" as the ones in our supermarkets. I also enjoy cauliflower cooked on the grill, but you need a basket of some sort so the small bits that break away from the head during grilling don't fall into the fire.

Cauliflower Puree

Simmer florets in a bit of milk and water until very soft. Puree it all, then add some butter, salt, and pepper. Served under a roasted piece of fish, this is so tasty and adds a very silky frame of elegance. Or simply add a bit of broth (chicken or vegetable) and it is a delicious soup. Garnish it with olives and anchovy (or not) and I will be home for dinner!

When it's in season, I bet I eat this once a week because it is soooo easy.

Roasted Cauliflower with Olive Oil and Flowering Thyme

Serves 2 to 4 (depending on the head size)

I always like to incorporate fresh herbs that are growing at the same time — which is almost all of them *all* season long. Flowering thyme is flavorful, and if you have it in your own garden or see it on the farm table, buy it. Scatter it on your finished dish. You can use it on everything. Otherwise, fresh thyme leaves are just perfect.

1 head of cauliflower
2 tablespoons butter
3 tablespoons extra-virgin olive oil, or more to taste
1 tablespoon balsamic vinegar
Salt and pepper
Flowering thyme

Preheat the oven to 400°F.

Leave the cauliflower root on and the lower leaves. This helps keep the head intact when you slice it. Cut thick slices (approximately ½ inch) with a really sharp knife. Don't worry about the little bits that fall off. Either save them and toss them into your next salad or roast them with your slices.

Set a rimmed sheet pan or large cookie sheet in the preheated oven until it is nice and hot. Pull the hot pan out of the oven and carefully add the butter, olive oil, and vinegar, mixing to blend. It will spatter, so be careful.

Place the cauliflower slices in the pan. Coat one side with the butter mixture and turn the slices over with a pair of tongs. Season with salt and pepper. If it seems a bit dry, add a little more olive oil.

Roast for 10 to 15 minutes on one side and then turn the slices over. It should be browned and caramelized. Cook for another 10 minutes or so, until the cauliflower is fork-tender. The timing really depends on how thick your slices are.

Transfer the cauliflower to a platter and garnish with the thyme flowers or whatever herbs you have. Serve hot or at room temperature.

Until I discovered this simple way of cooking it, I never really liked cauliflower. (I didn't like it steamed with cheese sauce, and I don't like it mushy unless it's in a pureed soup.)

Roasted Cauliflower with Aioli

I really like these flavors together. Cauliflower is very mild, and sometimes I want the added punch. This version in my opinion is a crowd pleaser, even for those who say they don't like cauliflower. It's also great at room temperature, which makes it easy for entertaining.

Follow the previous recipe but omit the balsamic vinegar. Also cut the cooking time by a third. The idea is for it to stay a bit crunchy, but not raw. It's nice to have a bit more crunch when eating it this way. (I am not a fan of raw cauliflower, but if you are, don't cook it at all, and use the anchovy aioli as your dip for it anyway. They are very good together.)

Sometimes I add a bit of toasted anchovy bread crumbs during the last 10 minutes of roasting. This is really, really good and gives it a nice crunchy texture. Omit the anchovies if you are not a fan!

To serve, arrange the cauliflower on a platter and fill a small bowl with plain or anchovy aioli to serve on the side.

Anchovy Bread Crumbs

2 slices or torn chunks of rustic bread
Extra-virgin olive oil
2 anchovy fillets
1 garlic clove, smashed

Preheat the oven to 300°F.

Place the bread on a sheet pan and bake for about 20 minutes, or until dried and crisp. Pulse in a food processor until the pieces are about the size of small croutons.

Heat a little olive oil in a sauté pan over low heat. Add the anchovies and garlic. Cook slowly, stirring occasionally, for about 5 minutes. Remove the garlic and anchovies. Add the bread crumbs and cook, stirring occasionally, for a couple of minutes over low heat, or until golden. Remove from the heat and let cool.

Aioli

Makes 1 generous cup

Aioli is a homemade mayonnaise that is delicious with fish, meat, and vegetables. Once you've mastered the basic technique of making aioli, you can create different flavors such as citrus (using more zest), anchovy, roasted sweet pepper, tarragon, and so on by simply adding the ingredients to the basic egg-and-garlic mixture.

4-6 garlic cloves, with the germ removed (see note)
1 large egg yolk or 2 small whole eggs
1 cup extra-virgin olive oil
Juice and grated zest of 1 lemon
Salt and pepper

In a food processor (or by hand), mince the garlic. Add the egg and blend until smooth. With the motor running (or using a whisk if doing by hand), *slowly* add half of the olive oil. Then add the lemon juice and zest. With the motor running, add the remaining olive oil, blending until thickened and emulsified. Season to taste with salt and pepper.

Crushing the garlic before chopping it releases the oils for better flavor.

Note: The germ is the little green shoot in the center of a garlic clove. Simply slice the garlic lengthwise and remove the germ with a small knife, because it's bitter.

Adding lemon juice to the egg directly can break down the protein in the egg and interfere with the emulsion process.

Always add your flavor variations — such as 4 to 6 mashed anchovies — in the beginning with the egg. This basic rule of adding flavor variations to the foundation applies to whatever you're building, whether it's an aioli, sauce, or soup. The only time you may want to add them toward the end is when using fresh herbs.

If you add something to the end of an aioli, it could "break." Then you have what we chefs call broken aioli. But even a screw-up aioli can be attractive on the right dish. Just like the molten chocolate cake, which originally was an underbaked cake. Everybody said "ewww . . . aahhh" — another screw-up that became a hit!

Roasted Farmers' Market Corn with Herbed Chili Butter
Serves 12

There is nothing better than fresh corn from the farmers' market. This is the only time I actually eat it. I especially love this for a barbecue, when you don't mind getting a little messy. But whether it's eaten hot off the grill or from the oven, it's delicious.

1 stick (4 ounces) unsalted butter, softened
½ cup mixed chopped fresh herbs such as basil, tarragon, and parsley
1 teaspoon hot smoked paprika
1 teaspoon crushed red pepper
12 ears of fresh corn

In a bowl, combine the softened butter, herbs, paprika, and red pepper. Stir until well blended. Peel back the corn husks and remove the silk. Smear the corn with the butter mixture and pull the husks back over the corn.

To prepare in the oven, preheat to 400°F. Place the corn on a sheet pan in a single layer. Roast for about 15 to 20 minutes. There's no need to turn it, but if you do, allow an extra 5 minutes or so of cooking time. Pull back the husks and serve.

If you're using a barbecue, keep the fire low so the husks don't burn. Be sure to turn the corn every few minutes. To serve, pull the husks back and shake off any charred areas. Place on a platter with the husks all going in the same direction.

To minimize the husks' burning on the grill, soak the corn — husks, silk, and all — for an hour or two before removing the silk and smearing with the butter.

Whole Roasted Duck

Serves 2 to 4

Anything cooked whole and on the bone tastes the best. For many of us, that idea can be intimidating or confusing. One of the most frequent questions I'm asked is "How do I cook a whole duck or goose?" You roast it low and slow, so it is succulent and tender.

Waste nothing — one of the best parts about duck is its rich, rich stock. Some duck stock in the freezer makes for a quick mushroom risotto or bean stew for another meal.

Duck is richer and has less meat than a chicken or turkey. If you are cooking for more people, it may be a better idea to buy 2 smaller ducks.

1 whole duck (4 to 6 pounds), rinsed and patted dry (giblets removed)
Moroccan Spice Rub (page 98)
Salt and pepper
Apples, quartered and cored
Turnips, peeled and cut into chunks
Thyme leaves
Butter
1 cup orange juice, preferably fresh (optional)
1 cup rich chicken or duck stock (optional)

Duck skin has a thick layer of fat, and you want that fat to be slowly rendered out during cooking. With a really sharp knife, make small (½ inch), shallow nicks in the skin all over the bird. Try not to pierce the meat. This is where people goof up — they cut too deep. If you do, no big deal, but you want to try not to.

Bring the duck to room temperature before roasting (20 to 30 minutes).

Preheat the oven to 200°F.

Rub some Moroccan Spice Rub into the skin and the slits. Season the cavity generously with salt and pepper.

Fill the cavity with a few apple and turnip pieces that have been seasoned with salt, pepper, some thyme leaves (save some for your sauce), and a dab or two of butter. Use just enough apples and turnips to fill the cavity. If the duck has enough neck skin, skewer or tie it to keep it in place, as you would with a turkey.

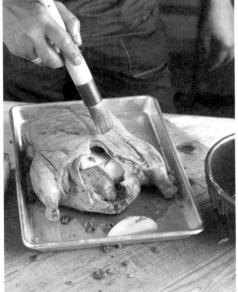

Place the duck on a rack in a roasting pan, breast side down. Roast in the oven for 2 hours. While the duck is roasting, periodically siphon off the fat. Carefully turn the duck over and increase the oven temperature to 350°F. Roast for another 20 to 30 minutes, or until the internal temperature is 135°F at the thigh (not touching bone). Remove from the oven and let the duck rest for 10 minutes; it will continue to cook to 140-145°F.

I think it's best to break down a duck before serving for easier handling at the table. First remove the apples and turnips from the cavity, then take off the legs, wings, and breasts, just as you would with a whole chicken. Or you can use a cleaver to chop right through the bones in large chunks if that's easier. You can put the leg/thigh quarters back into the oven to cook for an additional 10 minutes, or until done to your liking. Serve the duck pieces and the stuffing on the same platter. Keep warm.

If you want to make a sauce, transfer the roasting pan juices to a saucepan. Let sit for a few minutes in the refrigerator so the fat congeals a little on top. Then remove the fat or at least most of it. Bring the remaining liquid to a simmer over low heat and cook for just a few minutes. Add the orange juice and stock, raise the heat, and cook until reduced by half. Turn the heat off. Whisk in a tablespoon of cold butter and some fresh thyme. Season to taste with salt and pepper. Pour the sauce over the meat or serve on the side.

Baked Pears Stuffed with Chorizo
Serves 6

I created this dish when one of my farmers had so many different varieties of pears that I brought several home. They were out on my counter while I was cooking breakfast one morning, and I sliced one up and was snacking on it. As I browned chorizo sausage, I pinched a little for myself and found that the combination was really, really good. This dish will certainly perk up your brunch menu.

Alternatively, try this with a roasted acorn squash half. That and a salad is a fun supper.

1 cup fresh chorizo or your favorite sausage
3 pears or apples
Poached eggs, for serving

Preheat the oven to 350°F.

Brown the sausage in a sauté pan over medium heat, stirring to crumble.

Slice the pears in half and core.

Scoop about a tablespoon of cooked sausage and stuff into the cavity of each pear half. Bake in the oven for about 8 to 10 minutes, or until warmed through. Serve with poached eggs. Good morning!

Pears, Arugula, Pine Nuts, and Parmigiano-Reggiano
Serves 4 to 6

Arugula, a spicy salad green also called rocket, is best in the spring and fall.

4 ripe Bartlett pears (other varieties are fine as well)
Fresh lemon juice
Salt and pepper
2 bunches of arugula
Extra-virgin olive oil
1 tablespoon white truffle oil (see note)
2 tablespoons toasted pine nuts
¼-pound wedge of Parmigiano-Reggiano cheese

Core the pears and cut into nice bite-size wedges (do not peel). Place the wedges in a bowl, squeeze a little fresh lemon juice over them, and season to taste with salt and pepper.

Place the arugula in a bowl and dress with a drizzle of olive oil and a squeeze of lemon; toss to coat.

Arrange the pears on individual plates. Drizzle with truffle oil.

Garnish the pears with the dressed arugula leaves and top with toasted pine nuts. With a sharp vegetable peeler, shave cheese curls over the top.

Note: A little truffle oil goes a long way. It gives a woodsy flavor that's expensive but worth it. If you don't have any, you can substitute extra-virgin olive oil.

Red Wine Poached Pears
Serves 4

3 cups red wine (any red you like to drink will do)
¼ cup sugar
2 whole star anise
1 cinnamon stick
Pinch of salt
4 pears, preferably ripe but still slightly firm
2 tablespoons corn syrup or honey (optional)

In a heavy-bottomed sauce pot, combine the wine, sugar, star anise, cinnamon stick, and salt. Bring to a simmer.

Peel the pears, leaving the stems intact. Trim the bottoms slightly so the pears stand up evenly in the pan. Submerge the pears in the liquid. Keeping the wine barely at a simmer, cook the pears for about 20 minutes, or until tender. Remove the pears from the liquid.

Turn the heat to high and reduce the cooking liquid by about half, until it is syrupy. As the wine is reducing, taste for sweetness. If it isn't sweet enough, add corn syrup or honey.

Serve the pears warm or chilled, with the syrup.

Potatoes

Farmers' market potatoes are nothing like supermarket potatoes. The market tables are loaded with so many varieties. There are hundreds out there, all with their own unique flavor and texture. These potatoes are dug in the same season, probably the week or the day before they're brought to market. They taste like the *earth*, just as they should.

Supermarkets carry only a few varieties, most of which have been sitting in cold storage, who knows where and for how long. Many are likely to be last year's crop. There is no comparison between a supermarket "stored over" variety and the farmers' market potatoes.

Deep, almost nutty flavors are released from a freshly dug potato.

Smashed Potatoes with Olive Oil and Fresh Thyme

Scrub your potatoes. Leave the jackets on, as this protects them from getting waterlogged. Place the potatoes in a saucepan and add cold water to cover by about 2 inches. Add a good pinch of salt. Bring to a boil and turn them down to a simmer. If they are on the small side (silver dollar), the potatoes will take just 10 to 20 minutes. They will absorb some water. There may be a little left in the pan. If so, just drain the potatoes. Smash them gently with a regular handheld potato masher.

I go to my herb garden and pick a good handful of lemon thyme. I slide my finger down the stem opposite to the way it grows and then chop the leaves up a bit. Add as much as you wish — if you're like me, you love the flavor. Give it a few good glugs of the best-tasting olive oil, a little salt, one more go with the smasher, and *voilà*, you are ready to serve. No cream, no butter, just the honest flavor of homegrown potatoes at their best.

Sometimes I use other oils, such as hazelnut and walnut.

Because they have no cream and butter, you can make these ahead of time. In that case, I would wait to add the olive oil until just before serving. The olive oil is for flavor and moisture. You would lose both if you added it and then refrigerated.

This is a very unconventional way to make mashed potatoes. Some chefs would really turn up their noses at this one. What, no cream, no butter? I am also going to suggest that if you don't have an opportunity to go to a farmers' market to get your potatoes, skip this recipe altogether. It just won't taste the same. I like using purple potatoes for this, as they are not too starchy. German Butterballs are also really delicious.

Purple potatoes have a magnificent color. Place them alongside pink salmon and roasted cauliflower, and you have an amazing meal.

This recipe is so simple, but all the time people ask, "Why are these potatoes so good?" First of all, good food can only come from good ingredients. Second, it's not always the recipe, but rather the method you use. These potatoes are a good example of that.

Use any small potato you like. Pick potatoes of similar size. If you have bought them from one of your local farmers, you may have to give them a good scrub.

Butter-Braised Potatoes with Whole Garlic and Fresh Herbs
Serves 4 to 6

¼-½ stick (1-2 ounces) unsalted butter
1 pound potatoes
Salt
Handful of garlic cloves
Sprigs of thyme and rosemary

Remove the bottom oven rack. If your oven has a heating element on the bottom, place a rack at the lowest position. Preheat the oven to 375°F.

Melt the butter in a 10-inch roasting pan or ovenproof skillet over medium heat.

Cut the potatoes in half and lay them cut-side down in the butter. It is important that you fill up the entire flat surface of the pan. That way the butter won't be left hanging out there alone without a potato to absorb it. And don't pile them up — just one single layer is what you're after.

Salt the potatoes. Scatter the garlic cloves over the top. You can leave the skin on the garlic. Add the thyme and rosemary sprigs. Place the potatoes on the very bottom of your oven — right on the flat surface where you get the direct heat. This will ensure that your potatoes brown evenly and caramelize the butter. If your oven has a heating element on the bottom, place the pan on the lowest rack. Roast for about 30 minutes, or until crispy brown.

Pickled Celery
Makes about 4 quart jars

Last year I was at a farmers' market and bought a few stalks of the most beautiful long celery. Over the next few days, I ate one and wondered what to do with the rest. I decided to pickle them. This pickled celery is delicious with salads and sandwiches. Pickled green beans and asparagus are good, too.

1 celery stalk (approximately 7 ribs)
2 large carrots
1 red onion
6 garlic cloves, thinly sliced
5 cups water
3 cups white vinegar
6 tablespoons kosher salt
2 tablespoons black peppercorns
2 tablespoons white peppercorns
1 small handful fresh basil, torn
1 sprig of fresh thyme per jar
1 small sprig of fresh rosemary per jar

Pickling juice can be made in big batches and reheated over and over. Use the same ratio of water to vinegar to salt. Then, if you've got extra pickling juice, it can just live in the refrigerator, waiting for the next time you've got vegetables you'd like to pickle.

Clean and separate the celery into ribs. Cut on a diagonal into slices. Cut the carrots into julienne strips. Do the same with the onion. It doesn't matter really how you cut them as long as they aren't too thick — I like a quarter of an inch. Actually, the more random the cut, the better it all looks together. Combine the veggies and garlic in a nonreactive bowl and set aside.

In a saucepan, combine the water, vinegar, salt, peppercorns, and herbs. Bring to a boil, then pour the hot pickling liquid over your vegetable mixture and let it stand until cool. The hot pickling juice "blanches" the veggies, and that's good because they retain their crunch (texture). That is all they need.

Pack the mixture of celery, carrot sticks, onions, and garlic, along with some of the herbs and peppercorns and enough juice to cover them, into sealed glass containers. (I like glass just because it's pretty and I don't like plastic.)

The beauty of pickling this way is that it's really easy and fast and you don't *need* to can. You can store the jarred, pickled celery in your refrigerator. Or if you'd rather preserve it, you can process it in a boiling water bath for 10 minutes.

A Little on Sandwiches

I enjoy sandwiches made with a very few, very fresh items. My rule is no more than three or four ingredients. I think the less on a sandwich, the better. I do not understand the attraction of a sandwich piled high with everything but the kitchen sink. It is the American tradition of more is better, which speaks volumes about the tasteless food that we get used to eating.

Here are a few of my favorite combinations:

Grilled or seared albacore with olive tapenade, sliced fennel, and arugula

Thinly sliced steak with Vine-Ripened Tomatoes with Browned Sage Butter (page 62) and crumbled blue cheese

Grilled chicken with Tender Herb and Wild Greens Relish (page 95)

Prosciutto with goat cheese, sliced fresh figs, and mustard

Smoked salmon with thinly sliced Pickled Celery and Aioli (page 231)

The other important thing to remember is that whatever your ingredients are, slice them thin and use small amounts. If you are grilling, then take the opportunity to grill your bread or baguette. Crisp bread is always preferable, in my opinion. You can toast your bread in the oven as well. If you have a fresh baguette with a crispy crust, then maybe you don't want to grill it. That's fine. Sandwiches are so good when they have texture and are not so big that you can't get a bite with everything in it.

Cinnamon Rice Pudding with Caramelized Apples
Serves 4 to 6

⅔ cup short-grained rice, or for a lighter pudding, jasmine rice
3½ cups whole milk
¼ cup honey
½ teaspoon salt
1 cinnamon stick
½ teaspoon ground cardamom
1½ apples, peeled, cored, and cut into a medium dice
3 tablespoons brown sugar
Juice and grated zest of 1 lemon
1 tablespoon unsalted butter
2 ounces Calvados or other apple brandy
1½ cups cider

Rinse the rice in cold water several times, until it runs clear.

In a heavy-bottomed pot, combine the rice, milk, honey, salt, cinnamon stick, and cardamom. Slowly bring to a very low simmer, stirring occasionally. Cook until the rice is tender, about 10 to 15 minutes. Remove from the heat and let cool.

In a bowl, combine the diced apples, brown sugar, and lemon juice and zest.

Melt the butter in a medium saucepan over medium heat. When it's foaming, add the apples and cook until caramelized and browned. Remove the pan from the heat and add the Calvados. Be careful, as the brandy may ignite if the pan is hot enough. Let any flames burn down, return the pan to the heat, and add the cider. Cook until the mixture is syrupy and the apples are tender. Remove from the heat and let cool.

Stir the caramelized apples into the rice pudding. Adjust sweetness and salt to taste. Serve at room temperature or chilled.

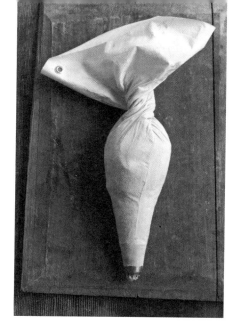

Churros
Serves 6 to 8

4 tablespoons unsalted butter
2 tablespoons plus 1 cup sugar, divided
Pinch of salt
2 cups cold water
1½ cups all-purpose flour
1 cup corn flour
4 large eggs
Peanut oil, for frying
1 teaspoon ground cinnamon
Your favorite chocolate sauce, for
     serving
Whipped cream, for serving

Special equipment:
Deep fryer, or a deep heavy-duty pot
Pastry bag and a big fluted tip (see note)
High-heat oil thermometer

In a small heavy-bottomed pot over low heat, melt the butter with 2 tablespoons sugar, salt, and water. Be sure not to let the water boil while the butter is melting.

In a bowl, mix both of the flours.

Once the butter has melted, bring the mixture up to a rolling boil. All at once, pour the combined flours into the liquid. With a wooden spoon blend carefully but quickly, until the ingredients have formed a uniform mixture. The batter will be very dense and sticky.

At this point, turn the heat off and add the eggs one at a time, incorporating each fully before adding the next. If you'd prefer, transfer the batter to a stand mixer with a paddle attachment and beat in the eggs one at a time. Once the eggs are fully incorporated, the churro batter is ready.

Pour 3 to 4 inches of oil into the deep fryer or pot and heat to 375°F.

Transfer the batter to a pastry bag fitted with a fluted tip. Working in batches, squeeze the batter out to the preferred length and gently ease it into the hot oil so you don't splash and burn yourself. Twist the churro as it goes into the oil to create a curly shape. As the churros turn golden, flip them with tongs so they cook evenly. When they are golden on both sides, remove from the oil to drain and cool on paper towels.

While the churros are cooling, mix 1 cup sugar and the cinnamon together and put it on a plate. Then gently roll the warm churros through the cinnamon sugar. Eat immediately with chocolate sauce and whipped cream. Yum!

Note: If you like them thin, a ½-inch fluted tip is the way to go for a long curlicue. I like them thicker, more like 3- to 4-inch doughnuts. This takes the biggest tip you can find — about 1 inch in diameter. The thicker the churros, though, the longer it takes to cook so that they're not doughy inside.

Simple pleasures are the greatest gift our life offers.
Savor each moment!

Fresh Organic
Chinese Chestnuts
in Burs

$6.00 lb

I am grateful to be living in a time when I must pay attention. We have all become more sensitive and knowledgeable about the fact that food plays a major role when it comes to our own health and well-being. The choices that we make affect our communities and the planet where we play and live. *TENDER* is the result of my own growing awareness through the years of how I can meet the challenges of making better choices.

We all lead busy lives and sometimes forget or feel like we don't have the time to spare to cook a healthy, simple, and creative meal for our family and friends. *TENDER* unearths the secret that only a few ingredients are necessary, that what grows together goes together, and that pure deliciousness and the success of the meals we prepare come from real food, grown and raised by those who are paying attention, our farmers. Taking time out of our busy days to shop at a local farmers' market is a simple way to bring joy and good food to our tables.

My hope is that *TENDER* will rekindle the spirit of community, connect us to those who nurture our planet — our farmers — and bring back the joy of simple cooking.

I am eternally grateful to those who made *TENDER* possible. To Jody, Nancy, Marlen, Angie, Patty, Judy, Tom, Norma, and all of our recipe testers, thank you from the bottom of my heart! I am truly blessed to be able to share my journey with you.

Tamara

aioli, 231
apple(s)
    caramelized, 250
    relish, 78
apricot(s)
    compote, 125
    grilled, with blue cheese and Serrano ham, 131
artichokes
    preparing, 30
    steamed, 30
    stuffed with ground lamb and almonds, 31
asparagus
    about, 23
    grilled, with arugula, poached egg, and Pecorino, 24

balsamic syrup, 132
barbecue sauce, Cuban, 89
basil syrup, 114
beans, dried
    in smoky white bean and ham hock stew, 225
beans, fava
    croustades, and mint, 41
    how to prepare, 40
beans, fresh, 150
    with anchovies, sweet peppers, and basil, 152
    pickled, 152
beans, shell, in risotto with spinach and
        bacon, 174
beef shanks, braised, 94
beets
    oven-roasted, oranges, and spring garlic, 34
    pizzetta, with caramelized onion, 157
Belgian endive, braised, 153
berries
    citrus–olive oil cake with, 117
    lemon curd with, 116
blackberry
    syrup, 120
    tart, fennel, 120
blueberry and goat cheese galette, 114
bread crumbs, anchovy, 230

broccoli, grilled or roasted, with prosciutto
        and roasted pepper, 138
butter
    browned sage, 62
    browned sage with hazelnuts, 197

cake, citrus–olive oil, with fresh berries, 117
cappelletti with browned sage butter with
        hazelnuts, 196-197
    with roasted butternut squash filling, 196
    with Swiss chard and ricotta filling, 196
carrot(s)
    in root vegetable mash, 204
    salad, Mediterranean, 33
cauliflower
    puree, 227
    roasted, with aioli, 230
    roasted, with olive oil and flowering
        thyme, 228
celery, pickled, 248
celery root
    puree, 207
    roasted, 206
    in root vegetable mash, 204
    soup, 207
chanterelle
    risotto, butternut squash and sage, 176
    soup, 161
cheesecake, mascarpone, with fresh apricot
        compote, 124
chermoula, 48
cherry(ies)
    salad, basil and mint, 104
    in stuffed morels with browned sage
        butter, 167
chicken
    in risotto, 172
    roasted, 170
chickpeas, garlicky, with Swiss chard, 199
chimichurri, 147
churros, 253

clams
    cider-steamed, with apple relish and chorizo, 78
    skillet-roasted, and mussels, 76
corn, roasted, with herbed chili butter, 232
couscous, fruited, 72
croustades, fava bean and mint, 41
croutons, 65
cucumber soup, minted, 127

desserts
    apricot compote, 125
    blackberry and fennel tart, 120
    blueberry and goat cheese galette, 114
    churros, 253
    cinnamon rice pudding with caramelized
        apples, 250
    citrus–olive oil cake with fresh berries, 117
    honey-roasted peaches, 122
    lemon curd with fresh berries, 116
    mascarpone cheesecake with fresh apricot
        compote, 124
    pumpkin steamed puddings, 187
    raspberry granita, 122
    red wine poached pears, 238
duck, whole roasted, 234-235
dumplings, ricotta, with peas, pancetta, and
        tomatoes, 56-57

eggplant, grilled, 141
eggs
    fresh, 18
    poached, 19
    with wilted frisée, 20
endive, Belgian, braised, 153
escalivada, 141

fava bean(s)
    croustades, and mint, 41
    how to prepare, 40
fennel
    grilled, 141
    salad, orange and olive, 106
    tart, blackberry and, 120

fish
    herb-crusted, with garden tomato sauce
        and summer vegetables, 60
    whole roasted, 100-101
frisée, wilted, with farm-fresh eggs, 20

galette, blueberry and goat cheese, 114
garbanzo beans, garlicky, with Swiss chard, 199
garlic
    in aioli, 231
    roasted, 148
    shoots, 47
gnocchi. See dumplings
granita, raspberry, 122
grapes, olives, and walnuts, roasted, 135

herb and wild greens relish, 95
herbs, in salsa verde, 107

Jerusalem artichokes, 212

kale, in smoky white bean and ham hock
        stew, 225

lamb
    ground, in stuffed artichokes, 31
    roast boneless shoulder, 98
leeks
    cleaning, 210
    creamed, with prosciutto and
        Parmigiano-Reggiano, 211
lemon curd with fresh berries, 116

morels
    cleaning, 165
    stuffed, with browned sage butter and
        cherries, 167
mushrooms
    chanterelle soup, 161
    cleaning, 162
    morels, 165
    morels, stuffed, with browned sage butter
        and cherries, 167

pizzetta, 158
porcini, grilled, with arugula and
    Parmigiano-Reggiano, 160
in spinach salad, 42
wild, roasted in parchment, 162
mussels, skillet-roasted clams and, 76

olives, grapes, and walnuts, roasted, 135
onion, grilled, 141

paella, 83-85
panini, grilled vegetable, 142
paprika, smoked, about, 215
parsnips
    fried garnish, 213
    in root vegetable mash, 204
    soup, 213
pasta
    cappelletti, 196-197
    with grilled vegetables and fresh herbs, 142
pastry dough. See shortcrust
pea(s)
    English, and mint soup, 68
    pistou, mint and basil, 68
    in ricotta dumplings with pancetta and
        tomatoes, 56-57
peaches
    grilled, with arugula and Serrano ham, 137
    honey-roasted, 122
pears
    with arugula, pine nuts, and Parmigiano-
        Reggiano, 237
    red wine poached, 238
    stuffed with chorizo, 236
peppers
    bell, in romesco sauce, 205
    grilled, 141
    roasting, 221
    sweet, soup, 222
pickled celery, 248
pistou, pea, mint, and basil, 68
pizza
    caramelized onion and roasted beet, 157

dough, 155
grilled, 156
wild mushroom, 158
porcini, grilled, with arugula and Parmigiano-
    Reggiano, 160
pork
    ribs, 88
    roast pig, 92-93
potatoes, 241
    butter-braised, with whole garlic and
        fresh herbs, 244
    in root vegetable mash, 204
    in skordalia, 145
    smashed, with olive oil and fresh thyme, 243
pudding
    pumpkin steamed, 187
    rice, cinnamon, with caramelized
        apples, 250
pumpkin
    puddings, steamed, 187
    soup, 184-185

radicchio, grilled, with goat cheese and
    balsamic syrup, 132
raspberry granita, 122
relish
    apple, 78
    tender herb and wild greens, 95
rhubarb, braised, 27
rice pudding, 250
risotto
    base, 173
    lemon chicken, 172
    roasted butternut squash, chanterelle,
        and sage, 176
    with shell beans, spinach, and bacon, 174
romaine, grilled, with anchovies and
    Parmigiano-Reggiano, 139
romesco sauce, 205
root vegetable(s)
    mash, 204
    roasted, 203
    storing, 201

rubs
  Moroccan spice, 98
  pork rib, 89
rutabaga, in root vegetable mash, 204

sage
  butter, browned, 62
  butter, browned, with hazelnuts, 197
salads
  carrot, Mediterranean, 33
  cherry, basil, and mint, 104
  fennel, orange, and olive, 106
  Niçoise, 103
  pears, arugula, pine nuts, and Parmigiano-
      Reggiano, 237
  spinach, with wild mushrooms and goat
      cheese, 42
  tomato and bread, Mediterranean, 65
salsa verde, 107
sandwiches, 249
  grilled vegetable panini, 142
scallions, grilled, 141
scallops, sea, with spiced orange vinaigrette, 71
shortcrust, rich, 121
skordalia, 145
soup
  celery root, 207
  chanterelle, 161
  cucumber, minted, 127
  English pea and mint, 68
  parsnip, 213
  pumpkin, 184-185
  smoky white bean and ham hock stew, 225
  squash blossom, 181
  strawberry Prosecco, 112
  sweet pepper, 222
spinach
  in risotto with shell beans and bacon, 174
  salad with wild mushrooms and goat cheese, 42
squash
  blossom soup, 181
  blossoms, about, 178
  blossoms, fried stuffed, 180
  brown sugar and balsamic, 193

butternut, 192
butternut filling for cappelletti, 196
butternut, risotto, chanterelle and
    sage, 176
fall and winter, 189
seeds, roasted, 193
spaghetti, 191
yellow, grilled, 141
stew, smoky white bean and ham hock, 225
stock, about, 216
strawberry Prosecco soup, 112
Swiss chard, 198
  with garlicky chickpeas (garbanzos), 199
  and ricotta filling for cappelletti, 196
  in smoky white bean and ham hock
      stew, 225
syrup
  balsamic, 132
  basil, 114

tart, blackberry and fennel, 120
tomatoes, 51
  bread, Catalan, 63
  herb-roasted, 53
  in ricotta dumplings with peas and
      pancetta, 56-57
  in romesco sauce, 205
  salad, bread, 65
  sauce, herb, five-minute fresh, 59
  vine-ripened, with browned sage butter
      and Parmesan curls, 62
turnip greens, in smoky white bean and ham
    hock stew, 225

vegetables
  grilled (escalivada), 141
  root, 201-204
vinaigrette
  basic, 47
  creamy mustard sherry, 42
  spiced orange, 137

zucchini, grilled, 141